I
WILL SURVIVE

I
WILL SURVIVE

MY PERSONAL FIGHT
WITH THE BIG C

BERNICE SWANN

authorHOUSE®

AuthorHouse™
1663 Liberty Drive
Bloomington, IN 47403
www.authorhouse.com
Phone: 1-800-839-8640

First published by AuthorHouse   12/22/2011

ISBN: 978-1-4678-8065-7 (sc)
ISBN: 978-1-4678-8064-0 (ebk)

Printed in the United States of America

This book is dedicated to all who fought and lost.

In the hope that something written here will help others find the something deep inside to fight and win.

CHAPTER ONE

I AM SITTING HERE ON THE 5TH OF JUNE 2011 WRITING this book, yet in August of 2010 I had found a priestess who could give me a pagan funeral and found and asked a dressmaker to make my shroud, I had wanted a full length dress with a hood and gone into town to find the material and been measured. To fall in line with my beliefs, I needed a materiel that was mainly red and found just what I was looking for, a red and Chinese dragon printed material and had it delivered. I had asked the dressmaker to do the garment by Christmas as I didn't expect to live past Christmas, but was still aiming to go to my sister-in-law for it. I was looking forward to my Birthday party in October and feeling pretty weak. I was dying of Oesophageal Cancer and I had all the treatment that was available. All I could now do was wait to die. Well I wasn't ready to do that so I was fighting with all I have in me. I thought I was fighting a losing battle but damn I have never given up when it really mattered, so I had no intention of starting now.

But I am getting ahead of myself. Here is my story.

*   *   *

I was born on the 30th of October 1949 in Stockport Infirmary Cheshire, to Dorothy Collins and Bernard Grayson Collins. My Mum wanted me to be called Lesley and my Dad wanted me to be called Bernice, so they put the two together and I was registered as Bernice Lesley Collins. I was the youngest girl of a family of five. I had two elder Sisters, Yvonne Avril and Glenys, and two brothers Roger Grayson who was only eleven months older and Steven Lawrence who was fourteen months younger. As there was several years between the older sisters and Roger, we ended up essentially as two families. We lived then in Rosemary Street Stockport, but my earliest memories are of a housing estate of Prefab houses in Whitefield, an area of North Stockport.

My memories of the houses were that they were the temporary housing put up to cope with post war shortages. While playing outside one day my younger brother Steven was run over by a coal lorry. There was a lot of shouting and panic going on; he wasn't hurt but what a kerfuffle. Dad took him to the hospital to get checked over, but he only had bruises and a couple of scrapes.

I can't remember the name of the school we went to. All I knew was it was a bus ride to get there. The school bus was a half cab with an open platform at the back and I was terrified of falling off when the bus set off so I was frightened of being the last one to get on the bus. One time the bus was late and every-one rushed on and I ended up at the end of the queue, I was terrified because I was then alone, the bus had gone without me. I started crying and didn't notice the bus returning, I had froze and was left behind. Then the conductress was there and she had got the bus to return and she placed me on the bus and got on behind me.

One day we were late getting up and we had to rush for the bus. I was so rushed I never put my panties on. No-one noticed until I did a trapeze act on the safety railing at the road side and a shocked teacher used a couple of safety pins to sort that out for the day. Mum was mortified and from then on she made sure I was fully dressed before I left the house.

We moved from Whitefield to a house in Cheadle Hulme. This house was down a little lane and it didn't have electricity. It was lit by gas and mum cooked using gas. In hindsight it should have been obvious that Mum wasn't too happy about the primitive nature of the cottage and I think this was the start of the breakup of Mum and Dad. The cottage was close the railway line and we used to go to see the trains go past. We took immense risks in those days but we were invincible and didn't worry about things like that. The estate next door was filled with trees and it was a great play area, we would climb the trees and play Robin Hood or similar.

One day whilst we were playing Robin Hood and his outlaws in the woods, Roger and the lad playing the Sherriff climbed one of the trees to a height of about 30feet. The daft kid playing the Sherriff stood on Rogers' hands and he fell, fortunately a branch lower down broke his fall but as it broke it also tore into his leg and opened it up to the bone. He felt at the injury and started screaming and we managed to get him home where Mum sent Yvonne to get Dad. Dad bundled him into the van and with Roger sitting on

Yvonne's' lap got him to the hospital where he was looked after but he ended up with a bad scar.

This was the era of the Teddy Boys and Dad said we must stay away from the areas they frequented. They were considered hooligans and not to be emulated. There was a place near a shallow river we used to play in and an area of demolished houses we used to explore and visit against Dad's permission.

Being the female between two boys I quickly learned to tolerate the obligatory worm, slug and creepy crawlies and to give as good as I got. I also learnt to climb trees and not be afraid of heights. That ensured I grew up more tomboy than a girl, having to fight for respect from two brothers, and this gave me the start of my fighting spirit and temper. This came into play one unforgettable Saturday when I and my brothers got up at dawn and snuck out with a couple of packets of biscuits for a day of play in the demolished houses and didn't get back home until nearly dusk and completely mucky from top to tail. Mum and Dad were so angry with us especially as Dad had told us not to go there because it was too dangerous. Dad said we had a choice of six of the best or being grounded for a week.

Quite naturally we chose the grounding; this lasted for just two days. Dad used his belt and us over his knee, Roger and Steven was first and I was tail end Charlie. For some reason this struck me as hilarious and I couldn't stop laughing. Dad gave me six but I didn't feel it, I was laughing so hard my ribs hurt harder than my bottom. I always had a weird sense of humour, and I never lost it. We were allowed out the following day, dad kept his word and we promised not to go there again.

Dad had a dog, a big German shepherd (Alsatian) bitch called Candy and one day I ran in to tell dad that another dog had hurt her cause she was screaming. Dad went out to see and found the other dog a Labrador, was a dog and she had coupled with him. Sure enough a little later she had pups which we loved. I found out then that Shepherds and Labradors breed true to type, and if you put the two together you generally get a full mix of what appear to be pedigree pups. Candy had 8 pups 4 looked just like Candy and the other 4 like their sire, a golden Labrador.

They caused a problem though and Candy was put into the coal house which my dad had made into a comfortable area for her and her pups, dad also modified the door which was made into a stable type door, the top half was able to be opened separately so Candy wasn't shut in totally. Candy was banished to the coalhouse because she kept putting the pups in Mum's side of the bed and mum didn't like that. My Granny Collins took a female Lab type and the rest of the pups were given away. At this time I think I was about five years old and felt happy and secure in a good family. Then my safe and secure family life fell apart. And until I married Brian it never came back.

We went to stay with Grandma Addys' for a while and then Granma Collins' for about a year. I don't remember much about Granddad Addy, I just have a picture in my head of a tall thin man with little round black glasses (John Lennon type ones) sitting on a dining chair next to the window in the front room drinking a cup of black tea in a large pint mug. He had a white stick in his other hand which indicated that he was blind. For some reason I really liked him, I felt safe with him, Granma Addy was tiny about 4ft 11, with her hair in braids on both sides of her face and a merry smile. Their house was a two up two down terrace, no bathroom just a tin bath we used in front of the living room fire. The only toilet was outside so in the night we used a chamber pot that was under the bed. We children slept in the second bedroom and Gran and Granddad slept in the front bedroom. We had to go to Granddad Collins because we got the flue and Gran Addy couldn't cope with that.

Granddad Collins I remembered was a medium sized stocky man always in a 3 piece suit without the jacket, and smelling of wet digestive biscuits. If I remember correctly he had a receded hairline until he was almost bald. Gran was the disciplinarian; she was plump but not overweight. Her hair was cut to the shoulder and she always had a ribbon to keep her hair under control. She was a great cook and because granddad had a veggie garden they were almost self sufficient in the food line. Their cottage was also a two bed and accessed from the main road via an unadopted lane. While we were at Granddad Collins we went to the local Primary School Edgeley Park, where it was us three against the rest, we had great fun.

Gran had chickens and ducks and used to boil potato skins to feed to them, I still remember this smell and it always takes me straight back. There was a big potting shed across from the house and all the feed and vegetable seeds and drying onions etc were kept there. One of the funniest episodes I recall was Granma killing a Chicken for Sunday lunch, Gran used to have a chopping block and she would put the neck of the chicken on it and with a small hatchet would take off its' head. The chicken often took off round the yard without it; we thought this was so funny. I never had any worries eating the said chicken for dinner. Granddad also had a number of garages on the property and we got to know the people who kept their cars there. I remember going shopping with Gran to the local shops and we had a wicker basket that we put the shopping in.

The shop was an old fashioned type that would cut cheese off a big wheel and sold butter in paper wrapped squares. Gran would also get her flour, yeast, soap, and cleaning stuff from there. Sometimes Gran would ask the shopkeeper to weigh 2oz of sweets for me and my brothers and he always gave us overweight so we had a reasonable amount to share. On a Saturday we used to go to the Market and get most of our weekly food that Gran and Granddad couldn't produce, like fish and vegetables Granddad didn't grow, Gran would sometimes get game like hare or rabbit and goose from there. It would all get put in paper bags and the wicker basket and we would go home and Gran would do some baking, including bread. Gran and Granddad looked after us very well but we were very young children and didn't worry about what trouble we got up to and more often than not we ran riot.

CHAPTER TWO

MY FIGHTING CHARACTER STARTED TO HARDEN WHEN I and my brothers were placed in Dr Barnardos children's home when I was about 7yrs old. My parents had separated, and my father couldn't manage us, mum had gone, where we didn't know. My grandparents were tasked with taking us to Barnardo's. We were in two homes during our stay there, the first in Chester. I knew in a remote way that mum and dad were no longer together but we didn't understand what that meant to us, just that mum had left and dad was not around.

Gran and Granddad took us there with no explanation that I can recall, we were just told to stay here at Boughton Hall and they would see us later. They never came back so the feeling of abandonment was high. Add to that I was separated from my brothers, and we were not 'together' for almost 6 years. I was able to play with my brothers during the day but at night I felt alone and unwanted. I used to sleepwalk whilst I was there and sometimes woke up tied to the bed. At first I was frightened and when it was explained I got angry and hurt that they would do that. The girls had dormitories of twelve beds but the staff brought us our clothes for the day. One momentous evening after we were put down to sleep, I decided to play trampoline on the bed mattress and fell face first against the iron bedstead and broke my two front teeth. Fortunately for me they were my milk teeth still. One of the staff came to see who was screaming and took me to the Matron who could assess the damage. She must have decided that nothing could be done so they gave me a warm drink and put me back to bed. The staff member who took me out of the dorm stayed with me until I fell asleep.

I used to spend my days alone reading or drawing, sitting on the window seat looking out into the large garden. I felt very alone, we didn't have our own toys and so I didn't even have a teddy bear to hug for comfort. My dad came to visit one day but all I can remember is he stayed such a short time I asked him if I could be a Nun and he said no, this was also the time when the orphans were being shipped to the colonies Australia and Canada. I asked Dad if I could go as well and again he said no, and wouldn't take us home, even though I cried. I never cried in company again. My wall was being built. I started to push the world away and learn to show only what they wanted to see.

The staff looked after us very well and didn't go into capital punishment but relied on trying to explain why such behaviour was not right. I retreated behind the wall for safety and so became sullen and stubborn and wouldn't talk to anyone including the other children. The staff would listen to our problems but I wouldn't open up 'cause all I wanted to do was go home and they couldn't do anything about that.

Gran and Granddad Collins visited one day and we were excited to be going out with them. They wanted to take us into town and we went to the bus stop, but we were on the wrong side of the road and so the bus went the wrong way instead of going into town. They took us back to the home and they never came to see us again. I feel it was about then that I nearly drowned in the swimming pool, as I was swept out of my depth due to the force of the water being pumped in to the pool at the shallow end. An adult swimmer caught me and took me to the side, and stayed with me until I got my breath back.

A few months later I ran away and headed into Chester. I just wanted to go home so I left the home after lights out. A policeman found me walking into the town centre and picked me up, and then he took me to the police station, where they alerted the home to come and collect me. My punishment was to not go out of the house for two days. I was also watched more closely all the time, so I couldn't runaway again. I don't recall going to school whilst I was there I must have because education is compulsory, but then I wasn't thinking of school only trying to understand why I was not at home. In all the time I was in Dr Barnardos I only saw my dad twice, and never saw my mum again. I didn't see my sisters until we left the home to go back to my grandparents' house when dad took us away for good in 1963.

I was not a "good" child in Barnardos; I was wild, stubborn, argumentative, sullen and willing to physically fight anyone. I quickly learned that if I let anyone know how hurt I felt they would make things worse. So my wall grew larger and I retreated behind it even more. I was more at home in my imagination so I ended up being a loner and not playing with any other girls in the home. I know I ran away at least twice, once in Chester and once at Barrows Green never getting very far and being punished for it. One morning we were told we were being transferred to another home in the Lake District. Six girls and seven boys were going.

We girls would be the first girls there because before us it was a boy's only home. In this home the boys and girls were separated completely and not allowed to play together except at weekends and only if we were related. In Barrows Green I did have some happy memories but they are few and they were mainly about riding the pony from the farm nearby. The pony was called William and was a 13h Dartmoor bay pony. I am afraid I cannot remember his owners name but she taught me how to groom and ride him. I rode him mainly bareback which taught me balance and came in very useful later in life.

That time was when I gained my love of horses and wanting to work with them. There was nothing personal with a horse or pony, if you hurt it, it would hurt you back. The time on the farm and with William taught me to be patient and learn how to read the body language of the animal. I used that patience in the home as I grew self sufficient with my own company. The farmer also had some shire horses for farm work and it was a great treat to be put up onto one of them whilst in harness to a harrow and ride him whilst he went up and down the big field. I held onto the brass turrets of his collar and felt proud and a little anxious, but he never broke out of his solid walk. The farmer at first kept fairly close to me in case I slid or it looked as if I was about to fall, but he soon saw I was comfortable and knew how to balance and go with the horses' tempo. It was a treat and my happiest times were when I was allowed to go to the farm for the day.

We had a Fete every year and one year we had the whole cast of Coronation Street come to open the fete, but I remember three of them best, Ena Sharples and her two sidekicks Minnie and Martha. We had a lot of stalls and a carousel, plus a Gymkhana and I was allowed to ride a couple of the ponies, including William. That was a good day for me.

We went to the local Junior School from which we were taught in rote the times table and mental arithmetic plus the usual curriculum. Every day in the autumn and winter we were given a Horlicks tablet to chew, I hated the taste so mine were generally chucked into the hedge bottom on the way to school. I was caught doing that one day and from then on I was watched like a hawk, and had to eat the hated tablet. The school was close enough that we walked to it two by two; boys in front and the girls behind with one of the staff walking there with us and returning to walk us back. We knew we were growing up when we were trusted to go without the staff member. We older kids went to school 5-10 minutes after the young ones started off. (The hated Horlicks tablets took residence in the hedge bottom again).

There was one incident that I still remember as if it happened yesterday. Going back to the home from school, I picked up a rabbit that was ill. I took it back to the home for Master Savage to look at and maybe help me take it to the vets. The Master took one look and got a spade which he used to kill the rabbit there and then. I started screaming at him, he told me the rabbit was in the final stages of myxomatosis and it would have died in agony in a couple of days anyway. I was sent indoors where one of the staff made sure I had a bath and my clothes were taken to the laundry in case any of the infection had transferred to me. I was kept in quarantine for a week. I still feel that day and it stopped the trust I had started to develop with him. From that date I started to seriously withdraw into myself and become emotionally self sufficient. I never let anyone else see me cry and I continued to build a wall between me and the world.

There was a lawned terrace that the girls used to play in outside. I used to sit holding my knees and staring into space for hours. I was lost in my own world, I would create myself into a Mountain Trapper or Scout, my name in my world was Flint McCullough who rode the plains and mountains of western America. I would create the adventures I went through living off the land as the Native Americans did, hunting deer and trapping small game to live. Or I would be a Greek or Spartan Warrior in the Trojan Wars. My imaginary world was more real sometimes than the one I lived in. In that land I was in control and it helped me find the strength to survive in the real world. I would take information about my imaginary world from books both fiction and fact and where I could, I would read avidly.

The other girls used to try and tease me until they found that it made no difference as I just ignored them. If they started to hit or push me for anything I blew up and I fought them as though they were boys. I won a lot of fights but also got a lot of punishment. The girls learnt to leave me alone. All my 'privileges' were taken away and I was confined to the house for a week, only allowed out for school and then under supervision. I don't know what chores the boys had to do but we girls were expected to do the housework and keep the house clean. The staff did the major work and the laundry, and we had a cook who was assisted by any of the children who wished to learn cooking.

We were expected to go to the chapel in the grounds which was a Methodist Chapel, every Sunday Morning and Sunday school every Sunday afternoon. One of the few times I saw my brothers was at church, but we were still not allowed to sit together. The boys sat on one side and the girls on the other. We were only allowed to sit together at school if we were in the same class or when our photographs were being taken. The rest of Sunday was reading in the girls lounge or doing other things like knitting or sewing. When we got old enough we were able to go into town (Kendal) to go to the Cinema if there was a suitable film on. I saw Cliff Richard in Summer Holiday one year, and was allowed to go alone by bus and return the same way. I was also taken to other families for the day or longer, I don't know why. I didn't know these people and the children were strangers to me. I always went alone without my brothers so it could just have been an effort to socialise outside Barnardos but if I did anything inappropriate I was punished and this 'privilege' was taken away.

I failed my 11 plus, but by so few marks I was asked if I wanted to wait and take my 13 plus and if successful go to Grammar School. But I found exams so stressful my mind would sometimes freeze and I would make silly mistakes. So I was not in the mental state to accept this, I refused and went to an all girls Secondary Modern School. We caught the school bus in the mornings but if we missed it going home or we had to stay behind at school, it was not unusual to walk home. There was a set of triplets at the home and one of them would often walk home with me. One of the girls made fun of me and my 'Beau' and because I was sweeping the dining room I used the brush to stop the teasing. Ma Savage came in at that point and I was put into a cupboard as only animals fought for nothing. And as I was an animal I should not mingle with people. I still had to go to school but now I was not allowed to get there with the other kids. School became my refuge and I worked hard to forget the home for the short time I was away from it. My favourite classes were Science, English, History, French, Geography, Biology, music and Art. I was in the top five consistently and did really well academically.

On Sports day I trialled for the One Hundred yards, unfortunately I wasn't fast enough. I didn't make any friends as they knew I was a Barnardos' kid and someone to tease, the other girls who were at the same school also got teased but I kept my distance and just ignored them and did more work to keep me at the top. I was at the point of choosing what subjects to take for my O levels when my dad took us out of Barnardos and I lost the choices.

CHAPTER THREE

T HE SCHOOL I WAS SENT TO REFUSED TO ALLOW ME TO follow my path. I wished to continue the science and go into chemistry and physics but *girls* weren't allowed to do those subjects.

In spite of days of arguments and discussions with my father he refused to let me change schools or take these subjects elsewhere. (I was seriously thinking of Veterinary School and required A levels in those subjects at least.) Dad was a traditional man who thought girls got married had kids and that was all. At that point I lost interest in school and only did the minimum necessary to stay in the top stream and my school reports were a round of "can do better, no interest", with the exception of Music, Art and History, until I left school at Easter aged 15 and a half. Did I give up? Well yes I suppose I did, but truth to tell my father would not help me financially to go to evening classes so that was out and that was that.

All we could do was Domestic Science and Biology. In those subjects I was ahead of the others in class, in some other subjects I was a few months behind. A good example of this was in the French Class. I was lumped in with other class mates who had gone up a stream and had never learnt any French, the teacher put a couple of phrases on the blackboard and asked what we thought they may mean. I put my hand up and answered in perfect French what the sentence said. I then translated it. The teacher asked how long I had studied French, I told her two years in an all-girls school. She asked why I didn't say so before. I answered that she didn't ask me what French I had done, but just assumed I knew nothing.

I was not popular with that teacher. She said my French accent was atrocious. (I will leave it to readers to decide who would know best about my accent). The teacher was Scottish and I was taught by a Parisian, who took us in French grammar and conversation. In that class we were not allowed to speak English, and I always got high marks in the tests/exams at year end. I ended up staying with the new girls and boys who had never taken French. As you may infer I got 99% in the end of year test in French. This was the same in most of my classes. That first year was all about revision for me.

I used to get into trouble in the Math class because I could get the answer in my head faster than working it out on paper. So even if the answer was right it was marked as wrong, because I couldn't prove how I got to the answer. The one Math I couldn't get my head around was Algebra. It just didn't make sense to me, such as Y + B equalled YB. I just couldn't see the values and although my teacher who was a very patient man, spent hours trying to show me, I never got the hang of it. I respected my Math teacher; I did not respect my French teacher. I recall that when we got a probation teacher, we were not kind to her at all, she didn't last long. We were shamed in Assembly as the headmaster named names and had us all take detention that day. I also got into a lot of trouble for fighting my brother in the playground. I had a lot of detention for being a hooligan.

My favourite class was the music class; it was in two parts, Theory and practical. I was asked to pick what instrument I wanted to play and I chose to play an Oboe, every-one else in my class picking the glamorous ones like violin or flute and clarinet. Being the only student to choose the Oboe, I was being taught one to one, and that made it easier to learn well enough to be placed in the Offerton Youth Orchestra. I was not only taught the practical but how to read music. I asked my dad if he could buy me my own Oboe, but dad would only buy me a violin or Cello, because he played the viola and thought the Wind section in an Orchestra not good enough. I had to give it up when I left school because I couldn't afford an Oboe and the one I had learnt on was a school instrument.

My years between '65 and '85 were not easy, Work was easy to get and my first job was in a lab for a Cotton Mill. It was a very noisy mill, and also very dusty. I stayed there for several months before I left and joined a one man Photographer in Manchester. I learnt to load cameras and develop film, and use a Gestetner machine that would print many photographs, similar to a photocopier of today. I learned to develop the templates on a thin sheet of copper, and how to ink it up for printing. He went bankrupt after I had worked there for almost a year, owing me a month's wages. My next job was in the Bellevue cafeteria. After that I was at the bookmaker William Hill; I was in the office using a comptometer. It was an adding machine that would work out the finance and how much was being brought in as bets. As an office worker I had to dress well and wore stiletto shoes, I felt a million dollars. Shortly after this my sisters had got married and left the family home. I remember my brother-in-law Phil and Yvonne came to visit on his motorbike and he gave me a great ride sitting behind him. He was wearing a helmet with a funny visor that had what appeared to be a fan that would spin and keep the visor clear in the rain.

I left home at 18 as I couldn't get on any more with my grandmother, if my Gran said black was white, according to her it was. Gran was never wrong. Add to that Gran was a great holder of grudges, and as I looked too much like my Mum she projected that grudge onto me as I got older. The reason for the Grudge was that during the Second World War, Dad was posted as missing presumed dead. Mum started an affair with a fighter pilot and had Yvonne. Shortly after, Dad was found alive in South Africa. His ship was cut in half and the half dad was in ended up there. Gran never forgave my mum for the affair. Gran and I were arguing so much it became impossible. So I left, with Dad saying don't come back with a bun in the oven, because I would not be welcome.

I got a bedsit in Edgeley where my current boyfriend joined me and we lived as man and wife for three months. Then we broke up and I left Stockport when I found I was pregnant and hitched it to Newmarket to work with the race horses. I loved the work so I worked there until my pregnancy became obvious, whereupon the trainer got me into a single mothers home in Cambridge. This house was run by the Catholics and I was branded as a sinner. We were supposed to attend Mass every day but as a non catholic I refused, which didn't help the situation at all. Mark Anthony was born after a labour of 36hrs and I felt very alone and scared. The staff at the hospital did everything they could to keep me calm and I always had someone close by to talk to. I returned to the home after a week in hospital learning to look after the new arrival where I was given a room of my own to stay in while Mark grew to be a beautiful baby of six weeks. I used to sing to him while I was feeding him and as the only song books were hymns I sang carols quietly to keep him amused. Yvonne and Phil came to see me and offered to take Mark and raise him with her children but dad said Yvonne was overloaded and it was not on. After six weeks a family was found and Mark was adopted, all I was told to do was sign the paperwork. The other girls said I was as hard as nails as my emotional self defence kicked in and I refused to show how hurt I felt. My wall kept growing and they didn't know how hard I was hurting and grieving for the baby that I had to give up. I had bonded with him and I loved him a lot.

I didn't want to leave the home with no job to go to so it didn't take me long to find a hunting stable who needed a groom and arranged to start when the home said I could leave. The stables were near Norwich and they employed me for several months. They taught me a lot of stable management, and I exercised the horses and under supervision, got the horses ready for the season. I left there just before the hunting season started because I wouldn't go hunting with the spare horses. It didn't help, with me not being able to drive. I worked on and off all over the south counties for two years. Within those two years I nearly committed suicide. I pulled myself away from the abyss and carried on working with horses. Finding myself pregnant once more I was sent back

to the home in Cambridge who really didn't want me there
so I was transferred to a home in Colchester. My second son
Darren was born in 1970 as a direct result of the attempted
suicide (my doctor at the time told me to get a dog or have
another child). Darren was two weeks late and made up for
this by arriving in 45mins from the first contraction. I had
intended to call him Dustine, but when asked what name
he would be I said Darren. This son was not going to be
taken away from me. So I refused to allow an adoption to
take place. The social Services found me a job where I could
take Darren with me.

I started to work as a live in carer for families with elderly
parents for about a year. I had kept in touch with My Gran
Addy and when I found myself out of work and homeless
with Darren she sent me a train ticket to Manchester and
I moved back to stay with her. She was able to help me
to look after Darren whilst I got a job to pay the bills
etc. Jobs were still easy to get so I worked as a Key punch
operator for the Great Universal Catalogue headquarters in
Manchester. The computer we were working with filled a
room all to itself; it was huge but was the cutting edge in the
early 70's. After about six months I left and went to work
in Weaving shed for Courtalds. It was closer and I didn't
have to travel so far. They trained me to operate two rows
of weaving looms. That winter I left to go home and almost
walked under a bus, I hadn't heard it. It was less than 100
feet away when I stepped out, but for the quick reaction of
a colleague pulling me back; I would have gone under it. I
resigned within the week.

In 1974 I got a seasonal job in Pontins as a Waitress for the
season, and my Gran looked after Darren. It was there I

met my first husband. My waitress nickname was Berni the Bolt after the TV program the Golden Shot. I also did what was known as the Chalet service which entailed patrolling the Chalets in the evenings to allow parents to go to shows and know their children would have some-one to listen for them, like child sitting at a distance, so if any child was crying I could alert the parents who had gone to a show etc. This brought me more money for the season as it was extra duties/overtime. I had to leave before the season ended because the Social Services contacted the manager to tell me my Gran was ill and I had to go home. Normally if you left before the end of the season you lost your bonus, but as it was a family emergency they paid me up to date and also paid the seasonal bonus. Mick was teaching me Wada Ryu a type of Martial Arts. I continued with this and it came in very useful later.

I was dating Mick throughout the season and he said he would come for me after the season ends. I had been back at Grannies' home for approximately 3 months, when Mick eventually arrived and we left when Gran was better. I married Mick a couple of months later. Mick was a good husband and then I got pregnant and had Sean Michael in August 1976 but he died in November of the same year to SIDS or cot death. The first week I couldn't stop crying. Eventually I lost three months of my life. My husband said I just sat and read anything I could get hold of, and only started to come to in January '77. Although Mick didn't blame me for the Cot death he changed and I really started to have problems. When I said I would leave him he said I wouldn't be able to as I had nowhere to go to and didn't have the guts to just walk out on him. How little he knew me, I had plenty of courage to do what I needed to do, and there would be nothing to stop me if I wished to leave. Later on that year I found I was pregnant again and I hoped I would be able to save my marriage. Then in the second trimester I started bleeding and when I went to the doctor, he said I was miscarrying. I was sent to the main hospital Kings Mill, where I lost my baby. The doctor said the baby wasn't growing right and if I had gone full term, the baby would be a Spinabifida, and he would not survive long after the birth. My body had aborted the baby because of this. Shortly after this I effectively lost my first husband, when he started hitting me instead of the wall and he also started an affair that combined to break the relationship between us in that year. I retreated behind my wall so Mick wouldn't know how I really felt. I walked out and went to a women's refuge in the North-East. My wall was well built now and I stayed behind it for a long time. I kept myself to myself and didn't tell the other women anything about us. We were all victims of Domestic abuse but I didn't talk about myself or why I was so far from my home area. It took Mick nine months to find me as he wanted a divorce. The refuge was in Grimsby and Darren and I had settled down there, and I was trying to find a job where I could take Darren.

When Mick found me he said he'd got the address from my brother Roger. He brought his new girlfriend with him which was why the manageress of the home allowed him to see me. We talked for several hours and Mick said he had applied to the court for custody of Darren stating that as I did not have a stable home Darren would be better served living with him and his new girlfriend, who he intended to marry when our divorce became absolute. I knew his new girlfriend and their two children who were close to Darren's age and this would be better for him. I told him to leave and come back the following day and I would let him know if I would fight for custody or not.

I sat down with Darren and talked to him about what was happening and asked him outright what *he* wanted to do and where *he* wanted to live. As he knew his dads girlfriend and had played with her children prior to her leaving her first husband and taking up with Mick, he expressed a willingness to live with them. I asked if he was sure and was happy to go. He said "yes please Mum" The following morning I told Mick that I would not fight for custody or divorce and if Darren was willing he could leave with Mick that day. I insisted that I would want visiting rights and this was agreed. I would keep in touch and when the court date was set I went down and gave up custody providing I could have visiting rights, this was agreed and I left Darren with Mick and Stephanie. Again my emotional self defence kicked in and no-one knew how much this affected me. I hid behind my wall which was now quite substantial, I survived. I turned inward and projected a calm and competent face to the world. I found a local stable near the Refuge and worked there for about a month, I would have worked there longer but they brought in a groom that had BHS qualifications, I didn't.

I returned to Norfolk and soon had a job in a land gang harvesting potatoes in Spalding. When this dried up I looked for a job in a local stable and returned to working with horses. I kept in touch with the court and with Darren; I was able to see him whenever I wanted. Darren had settled down with his new family and was not treated any differently from the other children. He and Damien his new brother were pretty close and they shared everything. Damien although he was younger than Darren, took the lead, and Darren was happy to let this happen. Mick and Stephanie wanted to adopt Darren but this I would not allow. I knew that sometime in the near future I would settle down and would want to regain custody again. Anyway I had already grieved for two sons and didn't want to go through that again.

My divorce absolute came on Feb 14 '78, whilst working in a riding stable and stud near Melton Mowbray. What a brilliant valentines' present. When that job finished I found a job in a Riding Stable looking after twelve horses and ponies. After about six months I left the riding school and started a job in a farm that had three great hunters. The owner didn't want me to go hunting with them just get the horses ready for the season and keep them fit during it. I left working with horses after the hunting season 78/79 ended and I moved back to Mansfield in March 79. The farmer said I could start with them again for the 79/80 season, but as it happened the job I got with the buses took me past the hunting season and I never returned to the horses. I had been learning to drive whilst at the farm and continued the lessons in Mansfield where I passed my test first time.

In July '79 I started a job In Mansfield as a Conductress on the local bus service. Because I didn't want anything to do with male drivers or conductors I was classed as a lesbian. I wasn't but I was not averse to leading them on about it. Then I met Brian and became friendly with him. But I kept him at a distance, and I didn't come out of my wall. He was married so it wasn't going to go anywhere romantically. Brian was a One man Operator and became my driver when my regular driver became ill and left. Brian was such a good smooth driver I got to know him well and started a relationship when he left his wife. I asked my landlord if Brian could have the spare room and he agreed. So Brian moved into my lodgings, and after a few weeks we lived together as man and wife. I applied for a council house so we could get Darren and it was approved. We moved in and I applied to the court to regain custody of Darren. To my regret I miscarried all other pregnancies and between us we continued raise Darren.

In early 1980 Brian wanted to see a lady he knew near Chesterfield and he told me she was in effect his mum, I was perplexed as I had met his mum and she lived in Sutton in Ashfield. Brian explained that she would have adopted him many years earlier but his mum refused even though he spent more time with them than with her. I met Jean Terrey-Kay that day and we got on like a house on fire. Jean was a Spiritualist and she confirmed that I was also seeing spirit. So what I had assumed was imagination all these years was factual. The weird feelings I had had when in certain areas was me feeling and hearing spirit. I started to develop this gift and also started to learn how to use the little healing ability I had. The following year Jean left for Canada and we lost touch for a while. I became a Spiritualist like Jean but didn't want to develop enough to become a working Medium. Brian had told me many stories about Jean and her first husband Arthur who had died of cancer in 1978, so I felt as though I knew them well. He had also told me of Mary and how she had looked after Brian when he had had accidents. Mary was a nurse and had helped Brian many times. Most of his stories were funny and we laughed many times over them. When Mary moved up north Brian lost touch and although he tried to find her he failed and thought he would never see her again.

We left the buses in 81 and joined a Taxi firm and worked for them for a year. Brian had applied for a divorce from his first wife sighting adultery. It was not contested and Brian got his absolute six weeks later. In 1981, I was driving a clapped-out old consul that needed the accelerator flooring to get it to move off even downhill when Brian told me he had sold the car and got another, he asked me to come out and look at it. The first words out of my mouth, was "take it back". The car was a Mk1 Capri, custom painted and set up for sprint racing, brakes and suspension up-rated, a full six cylinder works Ford three litre Essex engine, and had a reputation in Mansfield for being a car the police were interested in as a speed machine. The previous owner took our old car as a straight swap, because he was frightened of the power and speed of the Capri.

Thus started the wildest 4 years of car ownership I have ever had. Brian told me to take it for a spin before I decided. So I got in and did the same thing I have been doing for several months I put it in first, floored the accelerator and dumped the clutch. The next thing I was three hundred yards down the road in fourth and Brian was in the back. I pulled over to the pavement and Brian climbed back into the front and put on his seatbelt. How Brian ended up in the back is a mystery but the acceleration pushed me back into the seat and my gear changes were automatic. Brian just looked at me and smiled, "well do I take it back"? I just grinned, and taking it a bit slower indicated and drove off again. Because this was a powerful car, Brian taught me to drive both aggressively and defensibly, and how to handle the car at speed. He taught me to always look at well ahead in order to anticipate any problems that may develop. While driving the car a few months later I overtook an Escort RS and the driver decided to play, he overtook me and slowed down. When I overtook him again he kept up with me and prevented me from completing the manoeuvre, so I dropped back and pulled in behind him. He again slowed right down, at this point I was not only getting frustrated I was also getting angry. I again tried to overtake him and again he kept level with me so I just accelerated constantly looking across at him. He was grinning and waiting for me to again drop back but this time I just kept going. Two miles later and with the speedometer reading 110, I heard a bang. I immediately looked down to my dashboard but nothing was wrong and looking across noticed the RS wasn't alongside me anymore, his engine had blown up. My immediate reaction was to think stupid idiot and kept going at a more sedate pace.

I told Brian about it that night when he came home. The following week Brian went to a motor factors in town to get something for the Capri, when a young man came in and demanded to know who owned the black and gold Capri outside. Brian said it is mine and the young man immediately said he owed him a new engine, looking surprised Brian asked him how he reckoned this as he didn't recognise him. He said a bimbo was driving the Capri last week and blew up his engine. Brian said with an edge on his voice that that bimbo was his wife and had told him about the idiot who tried to race her and about what speed she was doing when the RS engine blew up, and if he was daft enough to race that car then it was his problem not mine. This wasn't the only time people underestimated my ability to control the car. Time and again sport car drivers would rev their engines along side of me at traffic lights, thinking that either the car was all show and no go or if it had the go I wouldn't have the bottle. I would just sit there in first, waiting for the lights to change and when they did I would just dump the clutch and go. Ninety nine percent of the time I caught them on the hop and showed them my rear end. I soon got the reputation of being a driver one didn't take for granted. Then came a darker couple of episodes, when one night I heard a knock on the door and upon opening it found Brian's' ex wife her new boyfriend with a long term acquaintance Wolfgang and his wife Kath there asking me where Brian was. I told them he was at work, no he's not I was told cause we have been there and was told he wasn't. I re-iterated that he was at work. Then Kath said Brian had raped her twice, and she was here to deal with it. My reply was short and sweet, I just said if that was true the police station was in town and she should report it to them not me. When the ex wife's boyfriend raised his fist, Kim my beautiful shepherd leapt over a sideboard straight for his throat. Fortunately for him I caught her as she passed me and I reckoned this was a good time to close the door. We haven't finished they shouted, you will hear from us again. I ignored it and went back into the kitchen where I was cooking my tea.

A week later I was driving into town and coming up to a set of traffic lights went for the brakes to find I hadn't got any. Fortunately there was no-one in front of me but an HGV was crossing from the right and I didn't think I could avoid him. Putting my hazards on and going down through the gears at full speed, I turned off my engine still in first gear hoping this would stop the car dead. I slid gently into the wall to the left of the lights and missed the HGV by inches. I sat in the car shaking like a leaf when the wagon driver came over and shouted are you OK and then what the devil did I think I was playing at. No brakes I gasped no brakes. Someone had called the police and it didn't take them long to get there, when I told them my brakes had gone, they checked the car and found my brake pipes had been cut. That meant malicious damage and the police asked me who may have been the culprit. I explained the episode of the last week and the bad feeling to my partner and I, they said they would investigate and get back to me as soon as possible. The police had contacted my partner Brian and he came over with someone to tow me back home, he was very concerned that it had been so close to a bad accident, and he thanked the wagon driver for being so considerate and helpful.

Brian had been taught by the Army to be mechanical and did all the work on the car himself, so it did not take him long to repair the brakes. Three weeks later we were woken up at 03.00 by the police who had caught Brian's ex wife's new partner under our car with a hacksaw. We sadly lost that car when we hit black ice and slid into a high kerb several years later.

My father contacted us in 1982 and asked if he could meet us to discuss some family business. My father, who had lost his second wife Enid to an aneurism, asked if I would consider coming home to help him cope. After a long discussion we said yes but I hadn't changed and would not be a skivvy for him, also my dog a beautiful Shepherd Bitch would have to get along with his. Dad agreed to our conditions and we moved up to the family home in Stockport that year. Dad had two dogs a rough collie and a toy poodle. The poodle was the randiest thing going and after having a seizure trying to couple with our bitch Kim, dad said we must get Kim spayed. I asked dad why his poodle couldn't be done but dad said the poodle was too old for the procedure. To keep the peace we got Kim spayed. Brian got a position as a tour driver with Shearing holidays and after a winter almost housebound with Sciatica, Mr Jackson the owner of Shearing's gave me a holiday in Spain with Brian. By the time I got back I had no sciatica, it had been baked out of me.

Darren went to the same school that I did, but got into a lot of trouble with bullies. When we complained to the headmaster about the bruises etc, we were told that Darren brought it on himself with confrontations. This came to a head when Darren was abused out of school hours by one of the bullies who tied him up and abused him so badly he had to go to the hospital. We were asked to let Darren testify and the abuser would be prosecuted. As it happened Darren was not the only case and he was relieved of needing to testify.

When Darren returned to school the bullying increased to such an extent we took him out of the school. The head and staff did nothing to help him. They just brushed it under the carpet, and according to them nothing was happening to Darren. Indeed Darren was in front of the head many times for fighting. We told Dad to leave Darren alone about this but he started to question Darren about it, and gave the impression that Darren had brought it on himself with his effeminate manner. Brian came in whilst dad was going on at Darren and Brian blew up. Then dad said something we were not prepared to tolerate, he told Brian that Darren wasn't his son, and so had no right to intervene. Dad and Brian had a big row, and we told dad we were moving out as soon as we could get another place. We moved when we bought our own home.

CHAPTER FOUR

W E GOT A HOUSE IN GREYSTOKE ST, OFFERTON AND moved in. Darren was placed in the local school and settled in. Brian was making enough so I didn't have to work, but I started a job in the petrol station on the main A6. When I was on the evening shift, my boss allowed me to have my dog with me. I worked there for about a year but when I foiled a robbery it was never the same. That was the only time my dog was not with me. Although my boss didn't approve of my actions, I felt unsafe at night, so I moved on and in 1985 I got a job in a factory making curtains and I operated an over-locking sewing machine. One day I stretched to ease my back and felt a painful lump in my right armpit. On feeling it, it didn't feel right, so I went to my GP who referred me to Stepping Hill Hospital who did a biopsy. What they did not say was the biopsy was a lumpectomy and they stripped the lymph glands also. The results were given to me as just a lump or growth, and I wasn't told if it was benign or malignant. When I asked, they said they didn't know. But they put me on a tablet known as Tamoxifen. I wasn't told it was a chemo drug. Because I was on sick leave, and no sign that I would be back soon, I was let go and so lost my job.

For six months I swung between "it was Cancer" and "I was over reacting". Brian could see the fear in my eyes but felt helpless and unable to do anything. It came to a head when he came home one evening to find me half drunk and a bottle of whiskey by my chair. Brian blew up and we had a full on row. I finally saw what stress he was under and threw the whiskey down the drain. I never drank again to combat the terror I was feeling. Instead I held it in behind my wall and dug deep into my reserves and got angry with myself for giving in. I got angry with the hospital doctor for not telling me the truth. I allowed Brian to only see my anger at the cancer and not the fear anymore.

In May the scar tissue started to thicken and swell and I went to my GP who calmly told me not to worry because the scar tissue would thicken up anyway. Deep down I didn't believe his blasé deduction, and went back to the Hospital Clinic and insisted on seeing the consultant there and then. At that point I was panicking and not in a stable state. The Consultant came and calmed me down and after an examination he confirmed that the lump was re-growing and referred me to Christies in Manchester. My appointment was in late September as this was the earliest they could see me and Stepping Hill didn't say it was urgent.

I saw a Dr Williams who became my consultant. He said the diagnosis was Cancer. My reaction surprised him as I said "thank you at last I know what it is that I am fighting". He was shocked and disappointed that Stepping Hill had not informed me or Brian of the results which was Breast Cancer. He also said the cancer was not the primary tumour. He told me I would have a series of Radiotherapies starting in a week and lasting 6 weeks. At the end of which I should have the Cancer completely gone.

To say I was scared was an understatement, but I now knew what I was up against and I did not automatically feel that I was a dead person walking. However, I was terrified of the disease, I had breast cancer and the survival rate was not high. My body was fighting me and trying to kill me. Still I faced 6 weeks of Radiotherapy and it would not be easy. So I got angry at the disease attacking me and my body for being such a wimp. Brian left Shearing and went to a local tour operator called Charterplan, so he would be closer to me and not away from home every night.

I went into Christies for the first treatment, the first thing they did was to tattoo a series of blue dots round my right breast area to aid the placing of the x-rays. I was under the treatment for 15 mins. at a time 5 days a week for 6 weeks. The first thing I noticed was the burning and redness which eased during the next 8 hours. The next treatment they put a cover over the treatment area, but the redness and burning got worse. As the treatments continued I felt tired and worn out. At the end of the treatments I was told I had only a tiny amount of cancerous cells left and the continuing work of the x-rays should kill them off. The hospital welfare sent us on holiday for a week to wherever we wished to go in England. I picked Plymouth and we were given a week's fully inclusive holiday plus some spending money.

I ended up essentially Piebald, with one breast the normal pale colour and the other sunburned and brown. This breast became solid and the ribs underneath became friable. They were weak and became easily broken. I suffered broken ribs just by coughing hard several times during the following ten years. I stayed clear of the Cancer for the next six months, and then the tumour started to appear yet again. At this point I felt as if I will never get rid of this and was very scared I might not beat it. Brian was brilliant in keeping my sanity intact, and helped in every way he could even if it was only a shoulder to cry on. In June of 87, I went back to Christies who put me on regime of Chemotherapy for twelve months. Brian had transferred from Charterplan to the Greater Manchester buses based in Princess Road Manchester when deregulation happened so he would be home every night. His new boss, the Depot management bent over backwards to help us, helping Brian to visit me in hospital and allowing enough time off to take me to the Hospital whenever I had an appointment.

I had two weeks of tablets and then injections of liquid chemo, and then a week off treatment. The tablets made me feel nauseous and the liquid chemo included an anti-sickness drug that just made it worse. The effects were accumulative and by the third month I felt very bad, constantly feeling sick and losing weight by the week. I was tired and weak and didn't want to move anywhere so I spent most of my time on a bed settee. It wasn't long before I didn't want to eat either. I began to have difficulty keeping solid food down and went onto Complan, a liquid feed that is supposed to give you everything a body needs (it tasted disgusting and I didn't want to eat it.) By the sixth month I weighed less than six stone, was very weak and tired, plus I snapped at everyone, even the dogs kept out of my way and I had about given up fighting. I was so tired and I couldn't stop crying.

I tried hard to drive Brian away telling him I didn't love him anymore and he would be better off without me, that I didn't want him to watch me die, but all he did was call his mum and asked her to come and see if she could put the fight back into me. Brian's sister brought mum down but refused to stay and went right back. I really cannot remember what she said or did but I started to fight again and carried on with the treatment. Mum stayed for about three weeks and chivvied me to doing little bits of housework trying to keep me moving and fighting. Thank you mum it worked. About this time we lost the house, and the council re-housed us in Adswood an Estate in Stockport.

The last treatment was the worst for me as I had been told the cancer was gone, but the last treatment would ensure it wouldn't come back. It took Brian, the nurse and Dr Wilson two hours to convince me to take that last treatment. Less than a week later I was seeing a physiatrist because I was suffering from depression. I was crying all the time and I couldn't get the pictures of the children under treatment out of my head. I knew some of them had died and I hadn't, I had difficulty coming to terms with this. It is called survivor guilt. She gave me some tablets that made me almost into a zombie, and Brian took them off me and I got myself better without them. I never went back. I retreated behind my wall again, and Brian accepted that I was better. That was what I wanted him to see.

The Chemo treatment had other long lasting effects in that it destroyed the enamel of my teeth and after advice from the Doctors I had 'em all removed and a set of dentures made. This was done at Christies in 1988. The Chemo also triggered the Menopause and I contracted Osteoporosis (brittle bones). I spent the rest of the year recovering and then we had an opportunity to Council swap and we moved down to Durrington, the weather was less severe for me in the South and I had family there. I was transferred to

The Royal South Hants Wessex unit under Dr Williamson. This is now March 89. At this point I had come out of the depression and I was determined to put the cancer behind me and live life to the full. As we were bikers we liked to go to the shows, I was looking to get my own bike in the near future so when I saw that there was a club for women bikers, I joined and found a friend that lived close to our new home. Jean soon became some-one I could talk to and we often went to the same shows for the next few years. Later that year we went to a show in Shepton Mallet, where I said I could take a turn on the WIMA stand. While I waited for my slot I wandered around the show with Brian, and we saw a helicopter that was taking the public around the show from the air. I didn't know it but Brian knew the pilot from his army days and he stopped to have a natter while I was on the stand. At the end of my stint, Brian took me over to the tent where the helicopter was and asked if I wanted to have a flight. I looked at the prices and said we couldn't afford it.

Brian said he knew the pilot and he was willing to show me around the cockpit and take me up for a short flight if I wanted to. Well this was a no brainer, I would love to go up in it but I didn't want to get the pilot in trouble. No bother he said it was all arranged and before I could say boo, we were airborne. The helicopter was the Bell Ranger and the cockpit had full visibility all round including the floor, I could see the ground just by looking down. It was fabulous, I loved it. It was even better when he started to throw the helicopter around doing stunts I didn't think you could do with them. When we landed after five minutes I had a grin from ear to ear. There was a queue when we landed but they only got the standard fly around. I think there were several disappointed people around. I was a member of WIMA for about six years until finances bit and I had to drop out of the club. But Jean stayed my friend in spite of leaving the club, and we visited each other on a regular basis.

Whilst at a clinic 3 months later, I was approached by a Dr Dianna Eccles, who stated that she was a Geneticist and was doing a study on early breast cancer in patients that were under 40. She asked if I would like to join the study and it would assist in the research of breast cancer and its causes. I agreed and a sample was taken and questions answered. Dr Eccles said she would get the results to me as soon as they were processed.

It took six months to get the results and it turned out that I was carrying the Breast Cancer Regressive Gene 01 (BCR1) and it was hereditary carried by the male line and comes out in the females. As Yvonne's family had this, it proved that it came down through Granddad Addy. I informed the rest of the family as soon as I knew myself just what I had. It took several weeks before it sunk in that I would be living with the knowledge that I could have breast cancer at any time from now on. I learned to live with this by putting it in a box behind my wall and putting the box at the back of my mind and throwing away the key. I learned how to do this at Dr Barnardos' homes. In this way I could cope with the loneliness and depressions.

No-one thought I was terribly unhappy because I learned how to put on a face that showed what I wanted people to see not how I felt. I used this ability to lock down my fears and show people a face that didn't show how insecure I felt. Most people thought I was a confident carefree person.

No-one saw the fear and the anger that I lived with not even Brian. It took Brian twenty years to make a gate into my wall. Even then there is a section that no-one has passed. My wall is a lot smaller now, but I can build it up very quickly if I get hurt from a trusted person.

In February 1990, we were asked if we wanted to go on the Elephantrefan, a winter Bike rally in Germany near the Austrian border. We jumped at the chance to go. The weather going was atrocious with gale force winds torrential rain and then freezing fog. The visibility was approx 10ft. After about 200miles we were overtaken by an articulated Lorry who had so many lights on his rig and trailer we were able to follow him to our turn off point to the rally. The rally was at Regensburg half way up the mountain. The temperature was well below freezing and there were plenty of bonfires to stand by and get some of the body warm. The mornings were beautiful as the mist lifted and the tents became visible.

It was a three day rally and we had really good fun trying to understand and being understood. There were a lot of people there and a goodly number came from East Germany, Poland and other countries that were previously behind the Iron Curtain. I had a fascinating time trying to identify the different types of bikes. One East German actually had a bike made from a lot of different bikes and the engine was lifted off a dumper truck. He said with a big smile that it was abandoned in a building site, so he rescued it.

It was fascinating and fortunately he spoke enough English to explain how he built it. I took many photographs and they are memories I will not forget. The game most of the men played was sledding down the slope on black plastic bin bags, hoping there wasn't a bonfire in the way. The daytime temp was approx—4c and the night temp was approx—20c. Throughout the night the bikes were fired up to keep the engines from freezing. That way none of us got a full night's sleep for the duration of the rally. On the second day of the rally the polizie organised a road race and all the fees went to a local children's hospital. There were trade stalls on the site and we looked around them but they didn't have anything we needed. On the last day we saw some late comers arrive, They were on 90cc step through bikes and they had come over the Alps from Italy, shepherded by trial bikes. You could barely see the bikes for the spares and camping equipment they had attached to their bikes. They definitely won the prize for the smallest transport, and I couldn't but admire their courage and sense of challenge for doing this rally.

The way home seemed quicker, but on the Belgium Autobahn things could have gone very badly as both me and Brian fell asleep whilst travelling. It took one of the other bikers several miles to wake Brian up and just in time as we were slowing leaving the road and going onto the hard shoulder. We pulled into a service station where we were plied with several cups of strong coffee. We reached home safely after that incident, happy but very tired. We promised ourselves to go again the following year, but we never made it and when the bike was stolen we couldn't replace it, so we never did go on another rally like it.

In June of 1990, I was told my sister Yvonne had cancer and wouldn't have long to live. To say I was in shock is an understatement. I knew by personal experience what she was facing and feeling also what the family was going through. Yvonne didn't want to see me because she said she didn't want my pity. How to explain that what I was showing was not pity but the remembered pain of what I went through. Yvonne died eleven weeks after diagnosis. Her cancer was because of something in the lining of her intestines not breast cancer (although I was to learn later that Yvonne did have breast cancer earlier but it was benign). I was devastated, I had just got to know my sister and I had lost her again. Cancer became a decease I grew to hate, as though it was a person who was attacking me and my family, and maybe that's the focus that helped me survive to today.

I decided I needed to retrain and find another career, and looked at office work. I didn't understand book-keeping and double entry so I went to learn to type and work on computers in offices. I passed my RSA and Clait, and started work on an NVQ1 on business administration. I got a post with a firm that did auto related items like carpets and embroidered clothing for local businesses and auto enthusiasts. I swapped from the office to the embroidery side of the business and stayed there for a couple of years.

Easter Good Friday 29th March 1991 and we are off on a two week tour of France and Germany on the GS. I wanted to go to Orange in the south of France and get home through Germany. We pack all the camping stuff, tent, cooker etc on the bike and set off for the ferry at Dover. We intend to stick to A and B roads and stay off the Motorways and toll roads; I want to see the country. The ferry journey was smooth as usual and after landing in Calais, we headed west along the coast road. The first night we stopped at a public campsite, the manager said that it was too early for most public sites to be open so we may not be lucky tomorrow to find a campsite available. The following day we continued west about 10K, when we saw a sight that beggared belief. On a cliff-top about 3k from the coast was a lighthouse. As we were between it and the coast we hoped the tides weren't too high, but could only surmise the coast had moved the 3k away from the cliff. Leaving the lighthouse behind, we continued on heading toward Bayeux.

Suddenly Brian stopped and turned round as he recognised the place we had just ridden through as Pegasus Bridge. We stopped there for several hours going through the museum and café and talking to Arrlette the lady that went through the time when our forces took the bridge the night before D day. It was a memorable time and when we continued on we promised ourselves we would return when we could. We stopped that night at another public campsite that had just opened for the season, it cost 7 francs and was the pits, the shower didn't work and the toilets were vandalised. We left the following morning and started south.

Around lunchtime we stopped at a hotel for food and a drink, and talked with the locals who asked why we weren't travelling on the Autoroute. We explained that we wished to see the countryside not the equivalent of the motorway. On hearing that, they gave some directions to the local sights and scenic roads and we talked some more before leaving to continue south. We couldn't find a campsite that night so I asked a man at a restaurant where we could camp, he said we could camp in the field on the other side of the hedge to the right of the restaurant but we must leave in the morning. We agreed to that as we were going to go anyway, so we stayed the night and continued south the following morning. Later that morning we stopped at a hotel for a sandwich and coffee, but after over half an hour and no sign of it we left and got one in a patisserie and ate it at the roadside outside the town.

As the afternoon wore on, we spotted a sign for a campsite 5k down a side road, 15k later we still hadn't found it and were just about to set up the tent at the roadside when we spotted a sign that said we were next to a defence base. We continued on and saw another sign 5k to campsite, Ok we went that way and this time we found it. Night had fallen by now and we set up in the dark. The nightly chorus of frogs had started up and we found this so funny we were collapsing with laughter, several campers came out to see what was happening and we had to explain what was causing us to laugh so much. The following morning we paid the fee for the pitch and bought some food to take with us.

When we reached the main road Brian turned south, it didn't take long to realise we were riding on the wrong side of the road when Brian said look at that idiot driving directly toward us. I said Babe we are on the wrong side not him. Whoops he said and we quickly moved to the correct side. Further down the road we got caught up in a tail back and it took over half an hour to move 200 yards.

This tail back was being patrolled by 4 motorcycle policemen who indicated to us to follow them. At first Brian declined as he was worried that this was a play for them to fine us for improper riding but after the 4th officer indicated us to follow we took the chance and followed them to the head of the queue and beyond. About a mile further on there were 5 motorcycle policemen in a lay-by and one of them waved us in. "here we go" said Brian expecting a load of questions and a possible fine, but all they wanted to know was what type of bike we were riding where we were heading and why. When we told them we were on a touring holiday through France and Germany they gave us information on where best to go for good value and stunning views.

We stayed in France going through some lovely medieval towns slowly heading toward the Alps and the German border for the next several days. One road we were on had a heart stopping optical illusion in that it appeared we would go straight through a big gate set into a tall wall, the road actually dropped sharply to the left. We soon entered a beautiful medieval town with very narrow roads and overhanging houses. A few hours later we reached the pass leading to Germany. We climbed this pass heading to Freiberg and when we got nearly to the summit we stopped and looked back. We were so high the cars and trucks looked like dinky toys. The view was spectacular, but we needed to get on and get into Freiburg before dark.

The trip down into Germany was out of this world, hairpin bends and no barriers. I can remember shouting at Brian to slow down as a couple of times we came so close to the edge I could see the bottom of the cliff. So a bend too fast and we would be taking the express straight down and no parachutes. That final part was definitely exciting. We reached Freiberg and found a campsite and managed to set up just before dark. Next morning we broke camp and started off to head toward the Rhine valley. We went through Boppard and spent the night at the Hotel Weinhaus Datt. Brian used this hotel on his Rhine Valley Tours and he was welcomed with pleasure.

Travelling on we found a campsite on the Rhine across from the Lorelie cliffs just outside of St Goar am Rhine, we used this campsite as a base for a couple of days to explore the villages nearby. Travelling on we reached Detmold where Brian was based when he was in the Army, here we would meet Gunter a landlord who befriended Brian in the 70's. Gunter was working in his bar with his back to the door when Brian walked in and called freigates Gunter. Gunter froze and then spun round and his face lit up. Brian he called freigates Brian. He walked toward us and gave Brian a big hug, he looked at me and asked and who is this? Brian put his arm around me and said "this is mien Frau Bernice, Gunter". Gunter shook my hand and said welcome to my home Frau Bernice. We stayed with Gunter for the rest of the day and Brian caught up with his news, it seemed Gunter's first wife Emma had passed away 10 years earlier and Gunter had re-married a younger lady called Krista who was now pregnant with twins. Not bad going for a 68yr old man.

When we left to return to our campsite that night I had passed Gunter's test but was as drunk as a lord. The following day I had a roaring hangover but Gunter gave me his pickup and told me to put it back in one. Looking at Brian he nodded and said it does work babe, so I did. Ten minutes later my hangover was gone. Promising to return later Brian took me to see the sights, including Herman's Denkmal a statue of an ancient hero who fought for Germany. The story goes that if Herman's Denkmal falls so will Germany, so it was a prime target for the RAF fighter planes who tried hard to demolish it. You can still see the bullet holes, but it still stood proud and a beautiful statue. We also went to see the Dams made famous for the Dambuster mission when our bombers broke the back of the German war effort. When Brian made a comment that you couldn't see the join, I think he upset a lot of local people and I expected to see him take the express elevator straight down. We certainly got a lot of frowns for that expression.

We said goodbye to Gunter and Krista and said if we could we would return and say hello to the twins, and then we set off for the ferry home. We started toward the Dutch border and got lost in Venlow, where a very nice lad on an old BMW Boxer gave us directions and then said follow me. He led us to the road that led out of town and stopped us in the middle of a six road junction to give specific directions. So there we were two bikes with cars buses wagons Uncle Tom Cobbley and all passing us from every direction. To say I was a bit tense was well very accurate; my heart was in my mouth the whole time. It was getting dark at this point so we didn't hang around, the ferry was due to depart at 22.30 and we had miles to go. Several hours later in the countryside a fuse blew and we were in the dark. With me pressing the brake pedal to warn any vehicles coming up to us, it took Brian an hour to get a new fuse and allow us continue.

At this point I asked Brian how far away from Calais were we, he replied about 150km, well I said we won't make the ferry, of course we will it's not far. So I asked when is our ferry due out. 22.30. We won't make it I said it's 21.45 now. When the air cleared we set off yet again. After about half an hour I got Brian to stop and told him I was hungry and would there be anywhere to get some food inside us. He said he would keep his eyes open and sure enough a short while later we found a picnic area where we could search our bike for food and a method to cook it if needed. All we could find was a packet of soup and some cheese slices, so we set up our little cook stove and made the soup in the pan. We ate it with the cheese slices doing service as bread. The result was so funny we started laughing and couldn't stop. About then a car and caravan also pulled in and a couple got out of the car. They looked across at Brian and I and promptly got back in the car and left. This was even funnier to us and set us off again. After we finished our meal we set off for Calais, hoping we could get on a ferry when we got there. Ten miles from Calais Brian dropped a bombshell when he said we had just gone on reserve, we just made the ferry but we were on the fumes. We coasted into the petrol station in the Dover Ferry Port and managed to get home with no further problems. An interesting trip with a few hilarious moments and plenty of memories and photographs to put into an album to trigger the do you remember this moment years later.

In 1992 I ended up with a prolapsed disc and spent the next 18 months waiting for an operation. After the op I tried to re-start my training in Business Admin and applied to Tidworth Royal Legion College to do an NVQ2.

This should have taken six months to complete. In March 1994 I found another lump in my left breast and went to the RSH Wessex Unit to have it examined. Jean came with me for a morale booster. A doctor did a needle biopsy there and then and told me to wait in the waiting room for a while. When I was called back after 30 minutes, the doctor told me he had found Cancer cells. For a while I was numb, in shock I suppose, I couldn't believe it was back again, and I was faced with the prospect of fighting it all over again.

I froze, tears falling and feeling terrified and asking myself why was it happening all over again. I had forgotten about the BCR1 Gene. Jean helped me get control of my feelings, so I could understand what the doctors were telling me, what my options in treatment were. One doctor said to another that I seem to catch cancer like most women caught colds; I was shattered, I could see me never being free of this damn decease.

I had an operation to remove the lump within the month and started a series of radiotherapy on a daily basis for another two months. Because I lived so far from the hospital they decided I should stay at Nettley Castle in Southampton for the duration. This was where the patients who came from the Channel Islands stayed when they were under treatment at the RSH for cancer.

Nettley Castle was a stupendous place, the rooms were beautiful as were the grounds and we were encouraged to wander and keep mobile. The dining room was panelled in wood and heavily carved and I felt as though I had travelled back in time. The food was really good and not bland. Whilst exploring the grounds I found a walled garden that was full of soft fruit. I asked the sister if I could plunder it for a pudding and was given permission provided a member of staff was willing to go with me. Between us we filled a couple of basins from the kitchen and we had a fresh fruit salad and a crumble that day.

Apart from the treatment sessions daily our time was ours to fill with whatever we wanted to do. I found the support of the patients and staff so good and Brian came to see me as often as he could, at least every other day if possible, and at the weekends Brian came over and we would walk on the beach. I did not feel alone and the fear could be held at bay. When I left Nettley I was clear of Cancer and I stayed that way for the next 14 years. Nettley was sold to a developer a couple of years later, which was a shame as they made it into luxury apartments for the seriously well off and unless you had an apartment you couldn't enter the grounds. The NHS and the Channel Isles lost a valuable asset.

I went back to college and because I had been ill I was allowed to continue my NVQ. Whilst I was there the Queen came to officially open the college. We were all briefed on how to behave if she came into our classroom and how to respond if she asked us a question. We were asked to dress as though we were in an office but not power dress (or overdress formally). The queen came into the classroom I was in and we did as requested and ignored her presence, I was overawed when she come over to me and asked what I was doing at that time. My tutor responded and said I was interested in wildlife and investigating a job in that area. The queen asked me what type of wildlife I was interested in particularly and I said otters and the smaller predators, followed by seals and sea mammals. The post I was looking at was for the Wildlife Trust who was looking for a part-time administrator for their office. She expressed the hope that I was successful and passed on to another class. That is a memory I will never forget and I have a photograph showing the Queen in our classroom.

On leaving the college I managed to enter an agency and did a lot of different jobs in offices all over my home area. This was an excellent way of learning how offices work and the type of office work I was best suited to. In 1998 I started work for the MoD in Andover within a registry and after 18 months they asked me to apply for the post and become a civil servant. This I did and started working for the MoD in October 2000 and stayed with the MoD to this day. I have made many friends and had a lot of support from my colleagues through my ups and downs.

In 1999 Darren got married to Tracy his girlfriend/fiancé. He was not long married when Tracy left him. Darren gained a flat in Bemerton Heath, where he tried to get his life in order. Both Darren and I were in Rehearsal for the Pantomime which the Amateur Dramatic in Durrington put on each year. This year the Panto was Robin Hood and the Babes in the Wood. Darren and I were playing the baddies who were supposed to do in the babes. I had left Darren at his flat on the Saturday after a rehearsal and he said he would come to dinner on the Sunday. When he didn't turn up for dinner, I tried to phone him but there was no reply. I went to rehearsal after dinner, only to find that Darren hadn't arrived. We contacted the police and they went to the flat to find the doors unlocked and Darren was found dead. The Coroner said he committed suicide but we have never accepted that as Darren had just come from celebrating a new job and a possible part in a professional play. Items were missing but the Police didn't see that that mattered. We still believe some-one killed Darren and got away with it. As you can guess this was not an easy time for me or my husband.

I was in rehearsal for the amateur pantomime, and Darren should have been in it too. I had to tell the cast that Darren had died but I would carry on for this one time. They honoured Darren by putting on the Pantomime in remembrance of Darren and his sterling work for the Drama Group. Again I did my grieving in private behind my wall. I left the Drama Group because with Darren gone I couldn't face going on. Mum and Dad came over from Canada in February 2000 and we laid to rest Darren's ashes. Mum had not been able to get here in time for Darren's cremation.

Mum asked us to take them up to her daughter Mary's house in Darton near Barnsley for her 25th Wedding Anniversary. Brian was really looking forward to that because he had lost touch with Mary in 1979 and had tried to find her several times since. Although Mum had known where Mary lived circumstances had not let Brian in on this and he was not happy to know that he had been kept in the dark. I don't know why this was but at last Brian will regain touch with his 'sister' and her family at last. Mum had phoned Mary to tell her when she would arrive and let her know that Brian and his wife would be coming also. After a drive of about 4 hours we arrived at Mary's house and I got out of the car so Mum and Dad could decant from the back seats. Mum and Brian went to the back door of the car to get the luggage and I waited so Mum and Dad could enter first. Brian told me to get in so I knocked and waited to see this crazy funny woman that meant so much to Brian when he was growing up.

Mary opened the door and I got such a great grin and a big hug I was surprised. I said "hi my name is Berni" and she said "yes I know, nice to meet you". When Brian entered the first thing Mary did was clip him across the back of the head, "that is for not getting in touch", the next clip was for losing touch. The next clip was for being lost for so long and the final clip was for anything else she had forgotten. Brian then got a great big hug. Behind Mary were her husband

Peter and her daughter Rebecca. I got a hug from them as well and Rebecca said "hi Aunty Berni nice to see you. From then on Mary and I got on so well I felt I had known her all my life.

Mary's son David came in later and Brian and I were introduced, he looked puzzled as to Mary calling Brian her brother, so Mary explained the relationship and how come she had not mentioned us before and they accepted us as part of their family. That evening we went to the venue for the party and had a lot of fun and laughs. There was a band and a disco, which unknown to me set off a serious migraine that night. The following morning I had a headache that kept me in bed. Dad came in and tried to lift the headache away but although it dimmed it, it didn't relieve it totally. I managed to come down for a bit but soon it rebuilt and I retired back upstairs. Mary came up and gave me some painkillers that sorted out her migraines but all that did was making me sick. The last day arrived and it was time to go home, Mum and Dad were staying as they were leaving for Norway for a short visit to Dads' son and then going home from Manchester. It was a shame that the visit was so disrupted for me but with Mary understanding Migraines so well she got me into the car for the journey home and asked me to a) keep in touch and b) come back soon. That was the first of many visits to Mary and she also came down to us many times.

In 2002 I moved out of the registry due to a managed move. I obtained a position in the Business group working on IT and Security for GWSS. In that year we had a Team Building session at a camp called Penhale in Cornwall. During that time I completed two of my ambitions. I did two abseils down the cliffs and over a cave mouth, and during one of the team challenges I asked the chief of staff if it would be possible to attempt the assault course after the teams had finished. I told him that if he said no I would understand and accept his decision. (He knew of my osteoporosis). He said if I would accept the team help he would allow it. The team, bless them agreed and with a little help I ran the course and finished it in good time. I was so grateful to the others for their help. It was a very good week. Later in the month I did a presentation on starting with the Project Team and what happened in Penhale, using the Team motto to tie it all together. The following year I was able to use up all my leave, to travel to see Brian's Canadian family.

Brian and Me

Phil and Yvonne

Brian's family in costume

With My sister and family

In my dream car

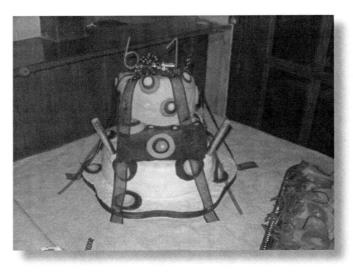

Birthday Cake.JPG

Niagra in winter

Back home

CHAPTER FIVE

W E HAD CONTACTED BRIAN'S FAMILY AND ARRANGED to fly out in the last week of June 2003 and booked the tickets on Canada Air. As we were flying from Manchester Airport we had asked Glenys and Alan if we could leave our car at their house for the duration of the holiday and they were happy for us to do that. So on the day before the flight we left home packed for the flight and travelled up to Glenys at Disley to leave the car. We stayed the night and Glenys took us to the Airport in time to check in. We gave Glenys a big hug and said our thank you's and goodbyes and she went back home.

This was my first flight in a jet and I was a little nervous, Brian found the right check in and we put our bags on the conveyor and gave our tickets to the check in lady. We passed through to the departure lounge and waited for our flight. Whilst we waited we walked through the duty free and bought some cigarettes and a couple of books. The flight was called and we went through the gate and boarded. Although I had requested a window seat the seat we had was behind this and the view was very restricted. The plane taxied to the runway and took off, it was not as exciting as I had thought it would be and I was a little disappointed but the flight was ok and although the leg room was a little cramped I felt calm.

It was a long flight and I really started to get a bit bored, the food was ok but not anything to write home about and not hot. We eventually got to Toronto and landed. It took some time to collect our luggage and we made it through the passport control. Mum and Dad were waiting to take us to their home and they gave us a big hug and helped us with our luggage. Mum and dad said we would be going to Halifax the following day as Dad was part of the Toward Clan and the Canadian Highland international games was on that week. Brian said are we flying? And mum said no we were driving there. That would entail a drive of over 1000 miles and would take 3 days. That was considered local in Canada as it is such a big country. On the way we would stop at Montreal and stop with some-one who needed Mum's help with a problem. We drove through a light traffic which dad said was rush hour and heavy. We said you're joking this is light traffic. Heavy traffic is nose to tail stop start stuff and this was not that. However we soon left the city and drove across Queen Elizabeth bridge and entered Hamilton. Dad continued until we started climbing the ridge that led to Stoney Creek and his house.

Mum and Dad's house was fairly large but only had two bedrooms. Their living and kitchen area was large and they had a basement that ran under the whole house. This was where they did their work with clients, and where Mum had her development circle. Mum was a spiritualist medium and a reverend and dad was also a psychic medium and they both did healing at home. As mum preferred to eat out we went to an Indian restaurant in Hamilton to eat that night. Mum and dad were welcomed with big smiles and we were given a beautiful vegetarian meal that wasn't too spicy and I really enjoyed it.

The following morning we piled into the car and set off for Halifax Nova Scotia. We stopped at Montreal for the day to help a friend of Mum's. Montreal is a definite French speaking city with tensions between the French speakers and the English speakers as the French speakers want to split from the rest of Canada, they have a name for them 'the Quebecoise' and it is not a polite one. We stopped with the lady named Michelle for the night after dealing with her problem, and we continued on to Halifax the following day.

The journey was incredible the sky just went on forever and the road was smooth and didn't stop. We stayed at a Motel in a family room where there were two double beds and an on-suite so we ate at the Motel restaurant and settled down for the night. The following morning we set off again and travelled through a forested area that didn't seem to end, the car never seemed to need petrol but I suppose we must have stopped and filled up at some point, but we seemed to travel for the full day without stopping until we pulled into yet another Motel. Mum had provided snacks for the day and again we ate in the restaurant. The final day we entered Halifax and Dad found the Motel we were booked into for the week. This time we ate in town and went back for the night.

The following morning after a good breakfast of pancakes and eggs, we set off for the field where the Games were being held. The weather was fantastic and very hot, and mum was concerned that we didn't get heatstroke, so tried to keep us well hydrated. We watched big brawny men in Scottish Kilts throwing the Hammer and tossing the caber, along with all the other types of games they seemed to enjoy hugely. There was a fantastic band of bagpipes and drums and I really loved the day. That night we went to the

International Tattoo and they asked for anybody who had served their country to stand and be counted. I got Brian to stand though he really didn't want to, but he had been in the army and he deserved to be honoured along with all the others. The displays were fantastic and it was a really good night, one to remember. The Highland games continued the following day and we watched the finals of the tossing the caber and the hammer throwing, the final act was a parade of bands and contestants with their trophies. Again it was red hot and I had a touch of heatstroke, Mum made me eat two packets of ready salted crisps and drink a litre of water to get me re-hydrated. I really didn't think it was that bad but I was dizzy and a little uncoordinated. There were a lot of stands selling things that people would like at the games and we bought a couple of tee-shirts with our Family Names on them. Most of the gear was just what one would expect and not worth buying as we were not Scottish and didn't need a tartan, we kept our money in our pockets.

That evening Mum and Dad said we were going to a Clan Re-union and we would be adopted into the Toward Clan, I wish we had bought the Toward tartan for that but we had name badges with the tartan on them. I had fortunately added a long plaid skirt and white blouse in my luggage and Brian had put a decent suit in his so we didn't disgrace Mum and Dad on the night. The dinner was excellent and there were speakers to entertain us and Mum and Dad had friends to meet and introduce us to. I suppose in reality I could wear the Toward tartan now if I wanted as a full member of the Clan. It was an interesting night and we went back to the Motel tired and happy. Next morning after breakfast we toured Halifax and visited the tourist sites including Pier 21 where the immigrants of the 1800's and

1900's were landed, and it was very interesting. The history was incredible and the displays showed what happened very clearly. Halifax is an interesting city and has a lot of very old building that are well worth visiting.

Our next outing was to the Thousand Island area of Nova Scotia and Peggy's Cove where we saw the lighthouse and the area where the airliner crashed. We ate at the seafood restaurant and had a beautiful meal. Brian was not allowed his favourite food, prawns as he is allergic to them so he had a fish dish that was delicious and he really enjoyed it. We went to a museum dedicated to a sculptor who had portrayed the fishermen and their families of Peggy's Cove and some of the sculptures were amazing. There was a montage outside that must have been over 40feet long yet the detail was fantastic, the people looked as though they would walk out of it. I took a lot of photographs and we had a really good day there. We got back to the Motel after dark and had a light meal before retiring for the night.

We headed back home the next morning. The journey back was as incredible as the journey to Halifax. There was very little traffic and for a lot of the time we were the only car. We stopped at a truck stop to eat and fill the car and I walked down the line of trucks until I found a driver who was happy to answer my questions on his Peterbilt 18 wheeler. He was just as interested in the way the heavy goods were dealt with in England as I was in Canadian trucking. I talked with him for about 10 minutes and I found him a pleasure to talk to. His truck was huge compared to the ones I was used to.

We stopped for the night at a Motel in Potato country and it was amazing that they were so proud of this fact. At the restaurant the following morning I bought a salt and pepper set that looked so life-like a potato my dog tried to eat one after we got home. (I found the pieces on the floor). Two days later we arrived at Mum's house and we settled in for the rest of the time we were there for. The following morning dad introduced us to Tim Horton's a fast food donut place that had all types of donuts you could imagine. I had a ball trying to decide what to have. We went to Tim Horton's a lot over the six weeks we were there. Dad had taken us to get water and order the water tanker for the Month, whilst doing that we visited a Tim Horton's place for a donut and coffee. I loved it and we went back as often as we could.

Later that day we were taken down into Hamilton and visited Mums' daughter and family. Ann was pleased to see Brian and welcomed me as a sister. Her house was pleasant and her family was fun to be with. We went out to the deck outside and had a meal al fresco with lots of salad and fruit, Ann is a vegetarian. Ann had a swimming pool at the end of the deck and she asked if I would like to swim, I replied that I hadn't brought any swimwear with me to Canada, she told me she had spare costumes there and was sure there was one that would fit. I found one to fit and went to the pool. As usual I just dived straight in and everyone was shocked. Ali and Ann joined me in the pool by climbing in via the steps. I have been back to Ann's house several times and seen Ann over here since we first went and they still seem to think that my dive into the pool that first day was something extraordinary and they still talk about it.

The following afternoon Mum told me I would be having a session of Reiki done by a gentleman called Bill, and I found a friend. That afternoon whilst I was outside, a very large pickup arrived with some quite large dark grey containers that looked like planters in the loading bed. This huge bear of a man got out and unloaded the planters as though they weighed only a few pounds. They were made of lead and must have weighed at least 300lbs each. Mum introduced us and the first thing he did was to pick me up and give me a big hug. I thought my ribs would break, he said "hi nice to meet you, name is Bill". That was my first experience with Bill Warriner. Brian admired his pickup and Bill tossed him the keys and told him to take it for a drive. Brian was gobsmacked and after quizzing him about the car, he got in and drove off for a drive round the long block. When he came back he had a grin from ear to ear. Bill took us all into the house and after a drink of tea; he took me into a room and gave me a session of Reiki. When I got off the table I felt woozy and Bill said take your time it will affect you for about 5minutes. After it I felt really good. That evening Dad said they were having a bonfire event the next night and I would meet some more of their friends and would get to know the people they deal with on a regular basis.

I was told by dad that he needed a licence to have a bonfire in his back yard as does any-one who wants an open fire in the open in Canada. The bonfire was built in a place where dad burns all his rubbish which is contained behind a small wall to ensure that the fire is reasonably controllable. As the day wound down people started to arrive and we were introduced to a lot of strangers with their spouses and older children. The people I remember most were members of Mum's development circle, Marcia, Patricia, Carol and Phaidra. Bill also came and so did Anne and her family. We had a picnic and toasted marsh mellows and had a lot of fun.

The following morning Brian took the riding lawn mower for a spin in Dads back yard. He was doing quite well until Mum came out and told him to come in because it was too hot to work. Brian being Brian argued the toss but Mum won and Brian came in. We went back into Hamilton to Ann's house where we had a music evening and so home to bed. For the rest of the week we went shopping and seeing Mum and Dad's friends.

One Morning Ann came over and asked if we had seen Niagara Falls yet and we said not yet, she said ok lets go and we spent the whole of the day at Niagara Falls and the town of the same name which was full of houses that looked liked the photo's we had seen of houses built in the 1800's. The following day we went to a town where it appeared as though time had stood still, like the Amish towns of America. It was fascinating looking in the shops that were full of old time things that my Great Grandmother would have recognised and they were for sale to the people who lived in this town and were in general use.

Two days before we were due to fly home Mum and Dad said we were going into the Indian Nations to witness a Pow-Wow. We went out of Hamilton and it took about an hour to reach the Nations. It was really special, the dances and music combined with the chants touched me in a way I haven't experienced since I went to see an Opera live. The clothes they wore for the dancing was out of this world and you could see they weren't doing this for tourists but for themselves. The atmosphere was electric and spectacle was awe-inspiring. There were some stalls selling goods they had produced and the work was outstanding, some of the sculptures were excellent but way out our pockets but hey we could dream. We bought some small items that we could afford and they were very well made, not tourist trash. We stayed for about three hours just taking in the atmosphere and watching the dancing, another memory to savour. That night we went to the Indian restaurant Mum went to most and had a really nice meal.

The following day we stayed close to the house getting ready to leave the next day. Ann came over and we talked and laughed about all sorts of things. Dad and Mum took us to the airport in the morning to catch the plane and we flew back to Manchester Airport. Glenys had given me a Key to her house so we could collect the car keys and make a drink if we wanted to, but we just loaded up the car, left a note thanking Glenys and Alan for looking after the car and left almost immediately. We reached home late that night to be met with delight by our dog Sam and Mina our cat. (A neighbour looked after them while we were away). I went back to work the following Monday. The rest of the year passed without incident until December when Brian had an accident at work and that put him off work for good. We had intended to apply to Canada for immigration the next year but Brian's accident put paid to that, we would have to stay in GB now.

Chapter Six

I WAS BEING CHECKED FOR CANCER EVERY 3 MONTHS FOR the first 5 years and then it dropped to every 6 months for another 2 years and then once a year from then on until 2005 when I was considered fully clear and no need for further checks. In spite of this I was checking myself every two months when having a shower.

In 2006 I got a feeling that something was wrong but nothing was showing when I was checking myself, it was mainly just a feeling. For the whole of 06 and 07 the feeling got stronger but nothing was apparent still. In 2008 I started having difficulty eating. At first I was chewing longer to allow the food to become small enough and soft enough to swallow, but by the latter end of the year, I was definitely having serious problems. I never thought of Cancer, I thought my dentures which were made in '88 were the culprit. I started thinking seriously of finding a dentist who would be able to make me another set.

Just before Christmas Brian noticed I couldn't finish a meal of steak and was cutting the meat really small to try to eat it before it got cold. He told me to go to the doctors because this was not normal. I made an appointment and managed to see my GP before the New Year. He suggested

I be referred for a Gastronomy scan. The earliest I could be seen was February and I went for an Endoscopic check. We were asked to wait for the results.

The Senior Nurse called us in to an office and gently told me that they had found Cancer. She said they needed to make a few more tests and I needed to have some scans to find out how developed it was and where it actually was. To say I was shocked was an understatement. I was numb; Cancer was the last thing I was expecting. At this time I told my line manager (who had just lost his father to the same cancer at Christmas), and explained I would need to have a lot of time off for hospital visits etc. He took that on board and arranged for me to work closer to home so I did not need to travel as much. My previous Project Team made room for me to work alongside them so I would be among people I knew and liked. They gave me a lot of support and ensured I did not overwork or tire too much.

I had 3 scans/tests in March and was referred to Dr Iverson in the Pembroke Suite of Salisbury District Hospital in April. Dr Iverson spoke to us and explained just what I was suffering from and that it was terminal as they couldn't operate because it was too close to the trachea. He said this was rare as most people who had this decease found it lower down the oesophagus. Although I felt numb the first thing I asked was how long I would have and would I reach Christmas. Dr Iverson looked a bit surprised that I seemed to take the news so calmly but he couldn't see inside me and see the iron control I was holding on my emotions.

Dr Iverson said I should see Christmas but my life expectancy was in months not years. I couldn't pin him down to anything more as he said each case was different and it depended on the person. How strong they were and how fast the cancer developed. He told me my options which weren't much, just the chemotherapy. He said I couldn't have an operation and because I had radiotherapy on each side due to the breast cancer I was unable to have that either. Apparently you cannot have radiotherapy overlapping and this is what would happen. He mentioned an experimental treatment in Exeter but I got the impression that that would not be suitable. At the time I could just about eat solids but I had to take care as the solids mustn't be too large. I was about able to eat small items and purees but steak and other types of meat were now out. I started to exist on soups and liquidized food. The dietician wanted me to start taking Fortisip liquid food, but I found them too bland and tasteless. I tried several other types of liquid foods but again I didn't like the taste. I was still able to eat normal food and I just made sure I could swallow it.

I needed some tests to ensure the chemotherapy would be alright for me and so it was June before the chemo started. As usual it was tablets and a drip and needed me to be in hospital for the day. My line manager was worried that I might be over doing it at work and really wanted me to go on sick leave right away. I wanted to continue work as it took my mind off my condition and allowed respite. I also had a lot of accrued leave I ought to take before going on sick leave. That month we lost our dog Sam who was almost 11 yrs old. That left us devastated as we had Sam from a young dog. However I couldn't grieve for long as I had to face the Chemo and would need all my strength for that.

I soon found that I could not take the tablets and after trying for 2 months to complete the chemo I came off that treatment. Dr Iverson was disappointed that I stopped the chemo and I asked him to contact Exeter to see if their treatment could help. This was at the end of July and I was about to go on leave.

I had promised my niece that I would attend her wedding on August 6th in Barnsley and to ensure that I would be OK for this I tried to eat as much as I could. I went shopping with Brian to get a suit for the day, and made sure he would not let me down I made sure he had a suit also. I found a nice suit in red that didn't cost a lot and looked reasonable so we went on to the wedding on the day.

The wedding was being held in the local Stately home. They had a chapel in the grounds and Peter led Becky to the table where the registrar was waiting to take the service, the music was played by Julian's cousin. Becky looked a million dollars in her Canadian wedding dress, and Peter was so proud leading Becky to Julian and when all the guests were settled, the service was held immediately. Whilst Julian was repeating his vows, Becky was saying very softly "Ball and Chain, ooh big ball and chain". How Julian managed to keep his nerve and not fumble the vows was remarkable, he even managed not to laugh.

The wedding photographs were taken in the grounds and only the group photos were formal. Becky and Julian wanted an informal set taken, so they disappeared for a while and the photographer took many photos showing Becky and Julian in various poses around the grounds. The rest of the family and friend groups had been taken throughout the gardens and the steps to the front door of the house.

The reception was held in the function room and the buffet was set up in a room next to the dining area. One of the caterer's came over to me to ask if I needed anything liquidized they would be able to give me something easy to take. However there was enough variety so that I had no problems. After the reception we all returned to the Hotel and we went to Arthur's house for the night. The following day we said our goodbyes and set off for home.

My manager was trying to work a sailing day for me and managed to get it for Aug 16th at Portsmouth using the Army sailing club. It was a good day and we sailed via the Solent to the Isle of Wight. I was designated the role of the Bosun and I was taking the tiller most of the time. The yacht was heeling (leaning) well as we picked up speed. Paul went below to make a drink; he managed very well and didn't spill much. It was my job to call out a change of direction (tacking), and as no-one got hit by the boom, I must have done reasonably well, and we had a good sail. We entered the marina and moored up with assistance from Guy our skipper who had had some banter with other sailors he knew. We disembarked and went to a good Pub and had a very good meal and I managed a thin soup. (The last proper meal for a long time). The day tired me out but I enjoyed the sail and we took plenty of photographs for the memories. Without realizing it I was eating and drinking so little I was slowly closing down organically.

CHAPTER SEVEN

A T THE END OF AUGUST I RECEIVED A LETTER LETTING me know Exeter wanted me to come in for the first treatment on the 7th September but then I received a phone call saying their equipment was down and they wanted to reschedule for the 3rd of October. I explained that I was now having great difficulty swallowing liquids and I thought that if I waited until October I may not be able to have the treatment. I was asked if I had had a scan recently and I explained that the last scan was the previous May. I was rescheduled for the 13th of September 2009. Brian called Mary and asked if she could come down for the time I would be under treatment probably a few days or a week. Mary found the time and came down the day before I was due to go to Exeter.

I entered the hospital in Exeter at 09.30 expecting to go home the same day. The paper work was sorted out with the ward staff nurse and I had an examination with Dr Toy who explained what was going to happen that morning and she told me exactly what the treatment was. I was told that they would put a tube through the nose and placed right next to the tumour, when a wire containing little beads of radio-active material would sit for about 3/4 minutes and that would shrink the tumour. The main risk would be that the trachea could be damaged or a hole made in my in my trachea or oesophagus. I was told that this treatment had been used in the States and Canada for about 15 years and normally used in addition to chemotherapy, so this was unknown ground and may not work. I took that on board and after Dr Toy left I settled down to wait for the call to go down for the treatment.

I went down to the endoscopy unit only to find they couldn't get a tube down. They said they would try again in the morning. By that time they found out just how dehydrated and how little food I had had in the last month, and I was becoming delirious. I started to demand to go home, but the nurses wanted me to stay so they told Brian and Mary to go and get something to eat and they sat and talked to me for an hour to get me to agree to stay. When Brian and Mary came back they took them to one side and explained what the problem was. Brian and Mary then also talked to me to get me to stay. At that point I was drifting in and out of consciousness and the seriousness of the situation was such that I was no longer protesting. I was dehydrated so badly, they put several drips in and they were in for 48 hrs. At the end of that time I was a little bit better so they decided to try for treatment again, using a paediatric tube but they still couldn't manage it, so I didn't get a treatment that day. I was told it would be better if I would stay longer so they could try and give me the 1st treatment 3 days later, I asked why they wanted to keep me in because I really wanted to go home, and they said that they could monitor what I managed to eat and drink and if necessary they could drip feed me. I agreed and they sent me down to have a feed tube placed through the nose and into my stomach. It was not pleasant and took a long time.

I had asked to be anesthetised but all they did was numb my nasal passage. I gagged so much it made it hard for them. I was so distressed I almost hit the poor doctor who was trying so hard. He said that screaming didn't help. I didn't realise that I was screaming but I certainly made a lot of noise. They eventually managed to get a tube in and I was fed liquid food. A few days later they used the feeding tube to guide a second tube in for the treatment. This time they were successful and I had my first treatment that Friday.

As I was so poor in health at that time, they decided it would be best if I stayed in until I was stabilised. I ended up being in Exeter six to eight weeks. At that point they decided the best thing to do would be to insert a peg feeding tube straight into my stomach, so after explaining what the procedure was and what it was for, I was scheduled for the procedure for the end of the week after the next treatment. The insertion of the peg meant I could get the nasal tube out. The relief was incredible as the tube went via the back of the throat and I was constantly feeling as though I would gag and be sick almost all the time.

I didn't realise just how close to dying I was, until I came round and found two vicars trying to give me the last rites. I am afraid I was not polite and told them to f* off, and said I was not ready to die just yet. They were, as expected much offended, but they really should have asked first. I appear to have lost some days because in looking back, the time line I remember is not consistent. Brian said I was in and out of consciousness for several days and had the drips in a lot longer than I recall. I must admit that my feelings were all over the place, most days I felt so tired and depressed. I was cheered up when I got visitors like Paula and Shann who must have bought up the flower shop they brought so many bouquets. Fortunately Exeter believed in flowers as cheering up the patients, many therefore got a bonus as there was too many for just my locker. My Auntie Rose and her sister also visited and she said she was shocked at how ill I looked. I did not feel that ill, I just felt tired. But from inside came the will to survive and beat this, so I concentrated on getting better. At that point my goal was to go home so I concentrated on that.

Mary stayed for the whole time I was in Exeter and for a week after I came home to help Brian cope. When I was released from Exeter I was asked if I wanted to go to Salisbury District Hospital or the Salisbury Hospice. I said the Hospice, so they arranged an ambulance to transfer me to the Salisbury Hospice where I stayed for a month. Again I set a goal of getting home, and the staff said that once I could manage the peg and my feeding and was strong enough I could go. After about a week at the Hospice I swallowed and instead of just staying put it went all the way down. My face must have been a picture because the nurse asked me what was wrong. With a great big grin I said it went down all the way, the nurse gave me a hug because she could see that it meant a lot to me. I was soon drinking a cup of tea normally and the staff soon realised I was getting better. Once the staff realised I could manage feeding myself through the peg and understood how to look after it etc, they let me go home.

When I left the hospice I could swallow and I started to eat almost normally, I was still on soft foods and meat was still out, but I could eat quiches and fish etc. This was good as just the fortisip was insufficient to build me up. At that time I weighed just 5 stone 3 lbs. I was too weak to climb the stairs in one go and had to rest half way up. I felt as though I was 99 yrs old not 60. My throat opened up a fair way for some time though I had a scare when some quiche didn't go down and I had to go to the hospital where the endoscopy dislodged the errant item and I was able to eat again. I returned to Exeter for more treatment, when I started to manage only thin soups and liquids.

I was still terminally ill and I started to make goals and I did an ambitions list of things I wanted to do before I passed away.

I wanted to visit my Mother and Father in-law who lived in Canada again before I went. I got there in January 2010. In order to have this, I returned to Exeter for another treatment. I had to go in on the Sunday to have the treatment on the Monday, I had another treatment. This enabled me to guarantee being able to eat normally in January and February.

We were invited to go to Mary's that Christmas and because of the treatment that month I was able to eat normally at Mary's that Christmas. That was the last Christmas dinner I had that I could eat the usual way. We loaded up with the presents and set off early morning. The neighbour promised to look after Mina for the duration so we didn't have to worry about her. We stopped at Moreton on Marsh to have something to eat, Brian went off to buy a sandwich and a coffee, whilst I got out my meds and food. I was half expecting the police to raid the car for drugs, because we had seen the reaction of passerby's. No-one came to look and see what I was actually doing, (can't get the staff nowadays). We reached Mary's early afternoon and after a cuppa we put our gear upstairs. We talked for quite a long time whilst waiting for dinner to finish. Mary asked how I was doing and I told her that I had had a treatment a couple of weeks ago and should have no difficulty in eating this time. We discussed the coming visit to Mum and Dad in January. The rest of the family arrived and we set the table for dinner. After dinner we chatted for about two hours then David and Rachael left for home. Becky and Julian followed shortly after.

Christmas day dawned and the presents were placed in the living room ready for the family to arrive. Mary and I disappeared into the kitchen to get the Christmas dinner on. Peter went to pick up his dad from Chesterfield and so ten of us sat down to dinner. Conversation was witty and the cracker jokes went down with plenty of groans. I managed to eat a reasonable amount as Mary had ensured that the meat was small enough and tender enough for me and Sid (Peter's father) to cope with. Wine was available and I had a small glass of the white and finished with a lovely pudding. I got away from the table feeling full and happy that I didn't need to use my tube. After dinner we all cleared the table then went into the living room to open our presents. We watched a film of the Simpsons which Peter liked, and we all had a laugh.

Suddenly I needed to get out of the house. I was feeling low and wanting to cry because I knew this would probably the last time I could eat a full Christmas dinner. I said I was going for a walk and left the house. I stopped just round the corner, and then Arthur came round and said "OK let's have a wander." He gave me a hug and we started to walk away from the corner. Whilst we walked Arthur started talking about anything that came to mind and nothing at all. Before too long I was feeling a little better and I found we had walked round the long block and arrived back at Mary's. I stayed outside and had a cigarette before going in. Arthur stayed for company until I went inside and then all was reasonable again. At first I found Arthur hard to read and was not too comfortable around him, but I soon realised that he was a kind and sensitive man who knew not to fear a connection. I am not a tactile person and I do not normally like people touching me too much, Arthur is very tactile and at first this is what was bothering me, but that was just Arthur and he didn't mean anything by it.

After tea Peter took a photograph of the tribe and then he took his dad home. I was sat on the settee with Brian on one side and Arthur on the other, both projecting support and sympathy until I felt a lot better. The chatter carried on until David and Rachael went home followed shortly after by Becky and Julian. Arthur followed a bit later and I went up to bed leaving Brian to talk with Mary. We stayed with Mary for another two days and then we went home.

Chapter Eight

WE HAD RECEIVED WORD FROM THE SPINAL SURGEON that Brian was able to fly again after a bad accident that damaged the lining to his spinal cord. So I told Brian to buy tickets for Canada immediately. After searching the costs we bought tickets to go from the 11th January 2010 till the 8th of February 2010 flying with Canada's national carrier. Because of the security aspects of the 9/11 restrictions on liquids we had to get clearance for my meds and feed going on the plane. We were advised to bring medical documents and a letter from the doctors that the liquids being brought onto the plane were not available in Canada and essential for my well being. So after letting Mum and Dad know the flight details we started to work out how much I needed of my meds and feed.

We had to factor the weight into the luggage limits so most of my suitcase was food and meds and not much clothes. With just enough food to last the time away we came in just under the maximum allowed. We discovered that if we paid the car parking online we would save a lot of money so that is what we did. We got the tickets and car parking tickets through Brian's e-mail address, and we started to get the packing sorted. We would be in Canada in the winter so a windproof and waterproof jacket was essential and I didn't have anything close to what we would need.

A trip to Salisbury was needed to get the jacket and anything else we felt we would need, so that Saturday we piled into the car and went to town. Knowing approximately what we wanted we went straight to the outdoor and camping shop in the Old George Mall and found a yachting type jacket that would fit me with a jumper on and we also bought some thermal socks and vests. Brian couldn't find anything there for him so we went to the Factory Shop in Amesbury where I had seen the type of jacket suitable for him. Brian found what he wanted there and so we were set up.

The day for the flight dawned and we put our luggage in the car and set off for Heathrow. After parking up we caught the shuttle to the departure area and went on to book in. We had to go through the security desks and I first off gave them the letter from my doctor and consultant so the meds and feed which I had in the hand luggage could be passed through without difficulty, the handler asked why I needed these so I showed him my feeding tube and explained that this was how I ate. We went through without problems and carried on through to the departure lounge. I had booked a window seat near a bulkhead so we had plenty of leg room and I could feed if needed. I had specified a soft diet which the airline thought meant a bland diet, not the same thing at all. I managed to eat some of the airline food but I left the plane in Toronto after going some eight hours without proper food.

Dad met us in arrivals after we found our luggage and started to leave the airport. We soon arrived at Mum and dads' home where we settled in and I had a feed to combat the hunger pangs from the plane. The temperature in Hamilton was -15 and the wind cuts right through one. I was surprised that there was very little snow there, in fact there was more snow at home than in Ontario. I was disappointed as I had been promised a play on a snowmobile, but there wasn't enough snow for it. The following day Ann came over and took us to Niagara Falls and we saw the falls all frozen over. The sight was amazing as the ice at the bottom of the falls must have been several feet thick. The spray had made fantastical ice sculptures of the railings and trees near the top end. Further downstream was an area where the river had carved out a large bay that creates a whirlpool when the river is in full spate. It was not visible that day but the place was incredible. Across from that was a large store where items made by the native Indians were sold. They also had a glass blowing workshop where you could buy one offs. There were incredible sculptures in wood on display and there were some beautiful jackets made of synthetic material that looks like reindeer or seal skin. Ann looked through them and found one that fit me like a glove. She threatened all sorts to Brian if he didn't buy it for me. It is hanging in my hallway now and most of my friends are trying to get it off of me, (no chance). Mum and dad were working whilst we were there so we didn't go out much, but we ate out a lot.

I only had two problems with eating, both in Restaurants, embarrassing or what. The first was with eggs; I asked for a very soft omelette and got a hard one because they weren't allowed to sell undercooked eggs and the other because it was so nice I tried to eat too fast. I learnt to eat slowly and it didn't happen again. I was still having problems eating properly but I managed some food in restaurants. Although we saw a lot of people and were involved in the development circle, we were essentially housebound unless mum or dad could take us out, so we watched the television and read. Mum was given films on DVD from a friend so we watched several films. Bill treated us to the cinema twice and we watched Old Dogs a good comedy with John Travolta as lead actor. There were many scenes where we couldn't stop laughing. The following week we went to see Avatar in 3D. We were advised not to sit too far back or in the closer seats at the front, so we sat in the centre rows and it was amazing. It was a brilliant film that I still remember clearly.

We went to Toronto to fly back and I hadn't any feed left, so when we went through the security for the departure gate, I didn't anticipate any problems. I had my letter from the doctor and hospital but the security wanted to take my Meds off me. I explained that I was under treatment for Cancer and the meds were essential for my well being, showing the letters I had used to take the flight to Canada. The officer was very suspicious and made life difficult as I had to show again the feeding tube into my stomach and explained yet again that the meds were liquid because I couldn't take anything else. I had to explain that the Morphine was on prescription and needed for pain relief. When Brian went through first they wanted to take his Sat-nav, then his car keys, and finally they confiscated his lighter saying that it was unsafe to go on the plane. After Brian managed to stop them taking the Sat-nav and keys, he said well I brought the lighter into Canada on the plane with no problems so why all of sudden is it not safe now? The officer just said it is confiscated and took it away. We finally managed to get through to the departure lounge with Brian muttering under his breath. We boarded and flew back during the night. Once again I was unable to eat the food the Airline served me and we reached Heathrow absolutely starving. We had no trouble getting through Customs and headed out for the car. Although the temperature was well above the Canadian Winter we had just come from we felt the cold as it was a damp cold. To make matters worse the car battery was as flat as a pancake and Brian had to ask for assistance. When we started to drive out the machine on the exit didn't accept the code we had been given and demanded nearly eight hundred pounds for the car park charges. Brian had to go into the car park reception who soon sorted the problem out and we were able to leave without further charges.

I had my last treatment in March 2010, where I was told that we were definitely in unknown territory with this. By May I was again having difficulty and went onto the peg feeding fully by June 2010. I kept on going and thinking about what I wanted out of my time, and brought out my ambitions list. In late June I received a call from Dr Toy asking if I wished to have a final treatment. I was told that the risks were now over 80% chance of damage causing a rapid deterioration and it could seriously shorten my remaining time. I discussed this over the phone and turned down the treatment, as the risk was too high.

My niece was playing in a concert, I wanted to go and watch her, and this would be in December. Following that I wanted to go to my Sister-in-law's for Christmas, therefore I must live that long in order to do it.

One of the things on my ambition list was a once in a lifetime drive in a 1929 Continental Bentley. I managed to cross this off as accomplished. This is how it happened.

In the 60's, television was considered a treat to watch and we were only allowed to watch certain programs. The one program I watched every week was The Avengers. The lead character was called Steed; he was a gentleman of the old order, who wore a pinstripe suit and bowler hat with the obligatory umbrella. He was the leader of a team of investigators similar to MI5 and saved England from the usual baddies using all sorts of things but steering away from guns unless they absolutely had to. Steeds' compatriots all had a fast modern sports cars that suited their personalities and so did Steed. His car was a 1929 Bentley Continental Tourer with a supercharger sat on the bumper just in front of the radiator.

It appeared as though the bonnet was 12 feet long, it probably wasn't but it appeared so. The bonnet had straps over the outside and the car was elegant and genteel and a wolf in sheep's clothing. Steed kept it immaculate and it could go as fast as the sports cars of his friends. Ever since I saw that car I wanted it. All other cars were judged against it and although I knew I would never be able to have one, this is my dream car. If I won the lottery this would be the first purchase. Of course I also had a slight crush on Steed as well, as he was the perfect English Gentleman. I have held this dream to own or drive one ever since (over 40 years I have been true to this).

I had told Brian what my dream car was many times when we were talking cars and comparing the different models as to which we would love to see on our drive or in our garage.

The 30th of September dawned as usual grey and overcast; I was looking forward to just another day, of watching television and reading a bit. Maybe working on the computer a little. Brian was in the study on the main computer, when

I heard him on the phone. The District Nurse had come to check I was alright and we were chatting about the cancer and its symptoms, what I should be aware of etc. After about five minutes the phone rang again and Brian answered it. He came into the room with a great big smile on his face. He told me that on the 5th of October I was going to get a dream to come true. Brian then told me he had had a call from Beaulieu and they had agreed to allow me to have a drive in a 1930's Bentley supercharged continental tourer. Brian was over the moon as he had asked at least two other people who had this car and got nothing but abuse from them. He said he had tried just one more before he gave up and that was Beaulieu. He had been put in touch with a lady called Helen Kiesel, who was the events manageress and she had got permission from the committee, and Lord Montague of Beaulieu himself has said yes. So the date was set.

The day dawned at last and my dream will soon be a reality, I am about to go and sit in my dream car, and imagine I am driving after some bad characters with Steed sitting beside me telling me to pour on the gas and watch out for that boulder or tree. I got ready and put on my yachting Jacket as that was the warmest jacket I had. (The car was a convertible soft top) we set off to go to Beaulieu.

Brian had been told to go through the staff entrance at the side of the main entrance, this was an electronic gate and Brian was given instructions on what to say in the speaker box. Brian was instructed to go and park in the arena parking area behind the main exhibition building and someone would come and meet us as soon as possible. Helen shortly arrived with a photographer who asked permission to take photographs of the day, I agreed and Helen then told us the car was in the workshop just round the corner having a service and general check-up to ensure there would be no problems with the drive.

Brian asked me if I thought I could walk that far but I didn't think I could so Brian drove round to the workshop. The car was on the ramp and I was able to walk all round it and have a good look inside, the mechanic said the car was ready to go outside and we watched as the driver slowly drove it off the ramp and backed it out of the workshop and parked up. I was introduced to Stanley who would drive me around. Stanley did not approve of the jacket I was wearing and gave me his driving greatcoat to put on over the top, he also said that today was a great day to drive out into the New Forest and thought that a two hour drive would be appropriate for the occasion.

I couldn't believe I was going to go so far and I was so happy I thought my grin would split my face in two. Stanley climbed aboard and after the photographer had finished taking his photo's in the area of the workshop we drove out heading toward the gate. As we moved off I saw to my right a couple who had a video camera and the man aimed the camera at the car, and filmed us driving out. The photographer took more shots of us at the top of the drive near a ruin and then we were off. Stanley was telling me all about how the car functioned and why this car was always in a road worthy condition.

They use this car for functions, events and rallies. This summer the car went to Monte Carlo for the famous vintage rally which they won, and returned to Beaulieu within 14 hours from Monte Carlo. They could not have dropped lower than 100 mile per hour the whole way and on the Autobahns they were topping 150 mph. Stanley told me the car would return 11 miles per gallon and held a tank of 80 gallon. Stanley asked if I was warm enough and informed me that the exhaust manifold was just above my legs inside the passenger part of the car. He said it was great in the winter but murder in the summer.

We went around the coast area and Stanley was not too pleased that he could not let the old girl out as the traffic was too heavy. This road he said is usually empty and he uses this road to open the car up and check the speed etc, and this was what he wanted to do but there was just too much traffic for some reason. He was not pleased, but I was content, I was having the time of my life. The sound of the engine and the feel of air round my face and hair were mind-blowing and just for a second I could feel how some-one could love the life style this type of car brought to mind, of 30's freedom and style of privilege and money. The power of the car was immense and I could feel the car wanting to speed up and be what it should. I wish I had been able to be in it when it was in a rally or race it would have been the trip of a lifetime.

We eventually found the gates to Beaulieu and turned in to put the car away for the rest of the day. Brian was waiting with Helen at the workshop and I finally climbed out of the car reluctantly. Brian had brought the wheelchair down and I got into it feeling tired but very happy. Brian talked with Stanley and satisfied his curiosity and walked away content. Helen said the Museum and grounds and house were open to us for the rest of the day and to contact her if we needed help getting to the house. We thanked Helen and Stanley for the care they had given me and we went round the museum for a couple of hours until I asked Brian to take me home as I had had enough and getting very tired. We drove home reflecting on the day tired but very, very happy.

Not long after that I decided my next goal would be have the party I should have had the year before when I reached 60. I would call it my 60+1 birthday party and we set about organising it. I sent out invitations to my friends and family and hoped about 50 people would be able to attend. The venue would be a local public house that could do the buffet and disco and not cost a fortune. As I had asked the disco to play 60's to 80's music only, I expressed a wish for the attendees to dress appropriately if possible. All I now had to do was live long enough to attend myself. At this time I could walk at most 10 yards without a struggle but any further and I needed to rest. So my husband would take me in the wheelchair for any distance. My weight was still under 6st. and I was pretty weak, but I was determined to make it to my only ever Birthday Party that I could remember.

During the run up to the party I was collating all those who could come and those who were unable to come so my mind was occupied and excited. I was not thinking about my condition and was concentrating on the party. My husband was getting other things sorted like the decorations. Unfortunately I was unable to get the right sort of clothes for the party due to my size. However some of the people said they had sourced 60's type clothing and would arrive dressed up. The party was a resounding success, The Stable bar was open for drinks and my sister, brother-in-law and niece all turned up in 60's clothes and wigs. My sister and husband arrived and stayed for the duration only going home the following afternoon. My 'surrogate' son and partner arrived with Damien bringing the birthday cake and it was wild. I loved it. There was a large buffet, and the Chef who cooked it all did us proud. The disco played what we had asked for and the music encouraged dancing. Julian and Becky did a Salsa demonstration.

About an hour into the party I was asked to say a few words to everyone and that was when Damien presented the cake with the Flares lit, My immediate reaction was to ask "what on earth am I supposed to do with that" and "are you sure it isn't going to blow up"? As the mike was live everyone heard that comment, and whole place cracked up, and as the laughter was contagious everyone was laughing. I said a few words and as I started to walk back to my chair, I found myself in a circle of friends and family who started to sing Happy Birthday. I laughingly threatened to kill them all for this. I kept in my wheelchair for most of the time just watching the others enjoying themselves. I never felt out of it as people came to keep me company and take me out for a smoke in the courtyard etc. We had great fun and I left with the party still going at 11.30 tired but happy. I went back the following day to pick up a couple of cakes including my birthday cake that was left. I told the Landlord to pass to his customers anything they wanted or do what he wanted with the rest. During that next week I bought and took to the Landlord a thank you card and expressed the wish that he thank the chef for his brilliant efforts.

I was on a high for more than two weeks after the party, and then Brian hit me with a treat I never thought would happen. On the morning of the 13th of November, Brian asked if I was up for an outing. I said yes and asked where we were going;

Brian said he needed to see someone about a possible spare for the Disco. We set off up the A303 toward Andover, when Brian said D**M I forgot the address and we turned around. When we turned off at the Thruxton turn off I looked and felt surprised and wondered what he had in mind. We turned into the Thruxton circuit and stopped at the offices. Brian said he needed to talk to someone in the office and asked if I wanted to accompany him. As I had never been here before I agreed and we got out of the car. We walked a short distance and then climbed a flight of metal stairs.

On entering the office I was faced with a form that required my signature, the receptionist said here you are; sign your life away just there. I gave it a quick read and found it was a membership form for something. Looking at Brian I raised my eyebrows in question form and he smiled and said its' OK. I signed and then she said "your pilot is just coming". I must have looked a picture, I turned and looked at Brian and said "Babe what's going on"? He smiled and said "Hun you goin to fly away". I was gobsmacked. I had been on a commercial flight and in a helicopter but never in a light aircraft and Brian had arranged for me to come to the Thruxton Flying School for a half hour flight, and the possibility of another flight in the stunt plane.

The Pilot, Steve took me to the Piper Warrior 111 and showed me the check plan prior to flight and how to get in and buckle up. Then he taxied to the runway and we took off into the sky. It was incredible; it was so much more in the moment and personal. I didn't take a camera so I have no pictures of what I saw but it didn't matter. The runway flowed toward me and then we were airborne. Steve said he couldn't fly over my house as it was in restricted airspace, but

I didn't care, we were flying and that was enough. We flew around some clouds which were too high to fly over and as we went round I looked at the cloud, the sun was behind me and our shadow was on the cloud totally surrounded by a rainbow, I have never seen anything so beautiful in my life.

Steve told me we would be flying toward Newbury and Highclere Castle a beautiful stately home often used in filming, and we also flew close to Aldermaston Nuclear Facility and the old airfield that used to be an RAF base. He told me what all the instruments did and how they were used by pilots flying the plane. He showed me all the maps and different screens on the console and what they were for. He told me how to turn the plane if I wanted but when I said I was happy just watching, he put it on autopilot for the flight home. I was so captivated by watching the instruments perform that I didn't take him up on me taking control, I don't regret that decision. He explained the final approach and the line that showed we were in the right place and what happened if he changed course and how to get back in line. I watched the whole of the landing procedure and it was amazing, we touched down as light as a feather. At the end of the flight I was given a photographic certificate showing I had had a first flight in that aircraft and when.

We had a chat with the receptionist who expressed an opinion that I was a daredevil. When I replied with a smile she talked about motorbikes and drag racing at Santa Pod. The information came out that one could be a passenger in a special drag racer for a small fee and experience the incredible thrill of the run at over 200 miles per hour. My Eyes lit up and Brian wailed "why did you say that, this daft one will want to have a go now". My grin just got wider, and this went onto the ambition list. I also said I wouldn't mind doing a wing walk but the docs wouldn't allow that. We spoke of different bikes and the runs we had experienced whilst waiting for the certificate then went home. It was definitely a day to remember.

A few weeks after this delightful adventure, we went to see Rebecca play in the Huddersfield Philharmonic Orchestra So on the 3rd of December, Brian loaded up the car for a 2 day visit to my sister-in-law's house in Barnsley. We needed a fair amount; my wheelchair, a box of feed and meds, I checked that I had water, syringes and 'micropore' (a sticky tape used to fasten bandages) I used this to fasten my feed tube to my body to keep it out of the way and out of sight. I also ensured I had spare tube and extension set just in case.

We set off in the car late morning aiming to get there in time for the evening meal. About an hour and a half later, we both got hungry and stopped for a meal. Brian made sure I was OK with the feed and such and he went off to buy a sandwich and take-away coffee. I did my meds and feed in the front seat half expecting a police officer to knock on the window and ask what drugs I was shooting. Both me and Brian laugh about this all the time. I had got used to doing a feed in public. After eating we set off again and reached Mary's home early evening.

Mary had got Brian's tea ready and put some of it into the liquidiser for me to have as close to their tea as possible. After tea we got ready to go and when Arthur arrived we all piled into our cars and set off for Huddersfield Town Hall where the concert was being held. Becky was already there and we were shown to our seats up in the gallery. We were told when we got there that the conductor had left suddenly due to ill health and we would see two interim conductors. I could see Becky who was in the violin section and sat back and enjoyed a really good concert. I was really proud of Becky for being good enough to be in the Huddersfield Philharmonic Orchestra. At the end we went down and waited for Becky and Julian to appear. We all went back to Mary's for the rest of the evening. We sat and talked until the early hours knowing we were only there for that one night, and had to be back home the following day.

The daily routine carried on with me feeding through the tube and having an argument with the Dietician about what could and could not go through the tube. I was still losing weight and unless I could up the volume I would never get enough calories to stabilise or even gain a little weight. I then told her that I was already putting other foods in just making sure that they were liquid enough to go in without trouble and ensuring no bits are in the food to block the tube. At that point she gave in and said just make sure you don't put anything too hot or acidic through the tube as these could damage the balloon that keeps the tube secure. I willing agreed to that and continued to think about what soups and other foods I could cook and how to manage the portion control. The last thing I want is to either waste food or overcook and Brian didn't always like what I could cook best for me. I was now an involuntary vegetarian and for an out and out carnivorous person this was not a happy situation. I had to work out how to incorporate meat into my diet and hit on the premise of using the meat juices and gravies and also using meat stocks in my soups. Just that I now have to ensure that there is no fat included as that could block my tube when it cools.

CHAPTER NINE

I WAS NOW LOOKING FORWARD TO CHRISTMAS AND I scoured the catalogue for good presents for the family and hoped they would come in time. Unfortunately some didn't so it was a quick run to the shops in Amesbury hunting frantically for presents to replace what wasn't here in time. Then another blow when the Catalogue sent out a recall on my Sister's present. I had picked a silver bracelet which I knew Mary could wear, but it had been mislabelled and was actually silver plate. I phoned Mary and asked her if she could wear silver plate and she said no. Damn, I didn't have time to get another present so I took the bad present with me to show Mary what she should have had, and told her I would replace it as soon as possible.

Christmas Eve day at last, off to see Mary and Pete and the rest of the tribe today. Brenda our great neighbour had promised to look after Mina so we had no worries about her. Got a text from Nicky to ask if today is OK for a visit, and as she has not been for ages I said yes but please to come in the morning as we were going away today. Nicky came and we had a really good natter catching up on friends and news etc and having a laugh at things in general. Then surprise, surprise, got a call from Shann and Paula saying they were coming to visit if we were in. Good to see them at last as they only pop round now and again. Shann and Paula eventually left and we finally managed to load the car and set off for Mary and Peters' home at approx 15.30. This is going to be a four hour run up north and after Brian checked the car for oil and water we set the satnav and went.

We stopped at Morton-on-Marsh so I could have a feed and take my Meds and Brian could get a sandwich or something and have a cup of coffee. That done we set off again. We only stopped once more for a toilet stop and to get the final presents at Trowell Services on the M1. We arrived at 19.30ish, and my legs and feet were very stiff and swollen. We had a nice surprise as Dawn and Mick were there to see us and give us a Christmas present. The present was a pair of slippers in a box that looked like a box of Felix food. Brilliant present and I immediately put them on, they feel great and it wasn't long before my feet were as warm as toast.

Brian was given a bowl of pork stew and a little was liquidized for me to have, tasted really great but then Mary is a very good cook. We had a very good natter and watched some television before retiring to bed at approx 23.30.

Christmas Day dawned got up late, unusual that. I had slept fairly well so I must have been tired. I sorted out the presents we brought and put them in the piles for the various people. Mary had told everyone that dinner was being put out at 12.00 sharp so it wasn't long before the family started to arrive. Rachel and David arrived. Becky and Julian were expected at 11.30 and Arthur at 11.00. Arthur was just in time for dinner and Becky and Julian was a little late but as Arthur had to leave for work to arrive at 14.00hrs he said he would open his presents on Boxing Day so Becky and Julian would be able to watch. As I had had a first meal at 10.30 I waited until 14.00 before having the liquidised dinner that Mary had put in the blender for me. After dinner we opened the pressies and had a good laugh at what was bought and given. Every-one was happy at what I chose for them so that was OK. I was delighted at mine and so was Brian. Family photos was taken and the party started to break up at about 21.00 Watched a little TV then went to bed at 23.00.

On Boxing Day I woke up very tired because I didn't sleep to well that night so while I was hoping to go to Meadow-hall Shopping Centre today I got a feeling I wouldn't make it. The problem is that because the centre is so big, I would not be able to walk around it and would need a wheelchair. Peter was trying to source a chair for me to enable the trip. Arthur, having a wheelchair said he would be bringing it with him and I'd be able to go. We managed to go late afternoon, I needed to get a bottle adapter at Boots for the Morphine as it's too low in the bottle to fill the syringes. We got to Meadowhall to find the Sales had started and the place was heaving. It was also a case of spot the white folk there was so many Asian and coloured people there. I even saw a Muslim woman in a full Burka, how she could see properly is a puzzle, there is not much room for eyesight. Rebecca wished to go to Next but was disappointed to find it was closed. As Primark was next door to Next and was open I asked to go there as I would like to see if I could get a cardigan and handbag. I found a decent bag that had been reduced by half and a good thick wool cardigan that had been reduced by at least 45% so was able to spend less than £20 phew, Brian should be pleased. As Arthur had given me £40 for Christmas My half went on this. Brian didn't go round with us he decided to sit it out and have a couple of coffees, which was a good thing as Arthur took me round at full speed and Brian would not have been able to keep up. When we had got what we wanted we set off to find him, not easy, we ended up having to Phone him to find out where he was sitting. After finding him we set off home. Heavy traffic but made it in good time for tea. Arthur opened his presents and was very pleased with them. We watched a good DVD on how the earth was made and then watched the idiots of Top Gear playing the 3 wise men of the Nativity during which time Clark and Hammond dressed up in full Burka' to avoid the customs which ended up a waste of time as they seemed to know that they were on the road and welcomed them with open arms, (never mind Jeremy it suited you well). For the rest of the evening I watched a little television worked a little on the computer and read a little of the book I had brought, before heading to bed.

Home today, I hoped we would get off reasonably early but I didn't hold out much hope. We waited for Arthur to arrive as he was meeting Tracy who flew in from Canada today. I went upstairs to get everything packed and ready to go, to find when I got back down stairs that Arthur and Tracy had arrived. So we had a natter with them both and finally left at 11.30. The trip across the Wood-head pass was easy enough even though it was reported as closed we found it snowy but clear, and we reached Glenys and Alan at 13.15. As I needed a meal and meds at that time I tucked in and Glenys made us a cup of tea. We had a great hour and a half with Glenys and Alan who opened their presents and were delighted with them as I managed to get just what they wanted, thank the goddess; she showed me the right ones to go for. We set off from Glenys at approx 16.45 and had no problems at all until we were on the M42 where an absolute idiot decided to get back onto the motorway from the exit slip-road and nearly caused us to be in a 3 car pile-up. Fast reactions from Brian and the driver behind us meant he missed us by inches. (Phew close call). We stopped at the services on the M5 at 18.40 for a meal break, Brian had a sandwich and coffee and I had my usual and we got home safely at approx 20.35.

In November I started to feel as though I had turned a corner. The pain was not hitting me so constantly and I started to feel better. Each week I felt a little stronger, I was still unable to walk far and tired incredibly quickly but by January I was taking pain relief out of habit not because I was in pain.

I queried this with my GP who said it was best to keep on with the pain relief because they didn't want me to have any pain at all. I asked my Consultant to give me an appointment for a scan as for some-one who was dying I was feeling extremely well and putting weight on. She told me that this was not normal procedure and it may not show anything has changed. I said "that understanding this I still need to know what was happening", so an appointment was made for the following month. I had a CT scan and the results came through a fortnight later. As my consultant had predicted the only thing showing was the scar tissue caused by the Brachytheraphy with a shadow just seen within it. The main thing was it hadn't spread or grown, and my consultant said "I think you are in remission, but I need to check with other oncologists to make sure".

When my GP saw the scan and the results she gave me a big hug and said "you are in remission, I knew you could do this". The down side of this is that the cancer is still there, I am not cured, it is just gone dormant. Well after the initial euphoria I came back down and said "am I still terminal or what"? "We are all terminal" she said, "but you are going to live a lot longer than we anticipated". The following week I phoned Dr Toys secretary to give her the news and Dr Toy herself came on the phone, so I was able to tell her that I had had a scan and it showed that the Cancer was dormant. She was ecstatic as this proved that her treatment had been vindicated, she said "you have made my year" and requested if it was possible to get the scan and report sent to her. I passed on the request and hope that it was done. The treatment I have undergone was experimental and has left me with many difficulties, not least being unable to eat normally;

I cannot even swallow my own saliva and must express it into a tissue. This leaves me embarrassed and I hate having to do it. I am on a full liquid diet and struggling to keep my weight stable, never mind trying to put it on. Most people think soups and purees are ok but soups need to be liquidized and then sieved enough to go through a feeding tube and not damage the balloon that keeps it in place. Nothing can be too hot or too cold.

Imagine sitting at a table looking at a full Sunday roast of Beef, roast potatoes, Yorkshire pudding, peas, carrots, beans and gravy and knowing you will never be able to eat it, never being able to eat cakes, biscuits, hamburgers this is my reality. My food is on prescription and liquid and supposed to give you everything your body needs, some milkshakes and Custards made from full cream milk boosted with double cream in an effort to get the fats and protein coupled with the occasional soup when I make the effort. Even finding full cream/fat yogurts is not easy as all manufacturers make low fat products because that is what sells now. People check calories in order to slim but I check to ensure I am taking enough to try and put weight on. I have a carer who comes in the mornings to help me have a shower and get dressed as the mornings are particularly difficult. If I don't sleep too well I am not good in the mornings. Some mornings I couldn't get up the stairs so I had a wash in the living room where I now sleep.

I have successfully fought off Cancer five times. How? I still don't know. All I can say is I am strong, stubborn and a fighter. I am in remission now but the fight continues as the cancer is still there and waiting to grow again. In the meantime I am living my life and trying to get back to work. I still have my ambitions list and I am working through them as finances allow.

So here I am sitting at my laptop on the 5th of July 2011 writing this book, yet in August of 2010 I had found a priestess who could give me a pagan funeral and found and asked a dressmaker to make my shroud, by Christmas as I didn't expect to live past Christmas 2010. I was dying of Oesophageal Cancer and I had all the treatment that was available. All I could now do was wait to die. Well I wasn't ready to do that so I am fighting with all I have in me. I thought I was fighting a losing battle but damn I have never given up when it really mattered, so I have no intention of starting now. Although I have a Damocles Sword hanging over my head I am doing what I have always done and I am just getting on with living the only way I know how, put it to the back of my mind, lock it in a mental cupboard and throw away the key.

I couldn't have done this without my husband Brian who gave me a shoulder to cry on and his foot up my rear when I needed it and the support and help from my family, friends, work colleagues and the staff and volunteers in both hospitals and the Hospice. Thank you all.

Lightning Source UK Ltd.
Milton Keynes UK
UKOW052113250112

186038UK00001B/40/P